W9-BYK-887

GAME ON!
MORE
Awesome Activities for Clever Kids

Patrick Merrell

DOVER PUBLICATIONS, INC.
Mineola, New York

Bibliographical Note

Game On! More Awesome Activities for Clever Kids is a new work,
first published by Dover Publications, Inc., in 2019.

International Standard Book Number

ISBN-13: 978-0-486-82467-3
ISBN-13: 0-486-82467-5

Manufactured in the United States by LSC Communications
82467501   2019
www.doverpublications.com

Have fun with this colorful, fun-filled book of puzzles! It is packed with a huge variety of challenges that include mazes, word games, jokes, spot the differences, word searches, mind-benders, and much more! Plus, this is the perfect boredom-buster for at home or on the go. All you need is a pencil!

In case you get stuck (or just want to check your answers), the solutions are at the back of the book, starting on page 121.

Coming Right Up

The answer to this joke is written using a simple code.

First, circle each letter that's immediately to the right of a V. We did the first one to get you started. Then write the circled letters (starting at the top and reading left to right) in the spaces below to answer this joke:

What do you serve but never eat?

B U X D O U M V (T) Q O B

V (E) N R Q W I O R W K J

O Y V (N) E M O U J B F W

V (N) N I Q U N Z U X Y U

B Q N V (I) U X O B S C E W

I G C Z M H Q E V (S) E T

E M I Q L J U K X S Z A

Z Q E N V (B) L P Z B M I

B S M N I X S R D Q V (A)

V (L) Q S L Z M G E D O Y

X M E V (L) E N R P I Z R

G B Z M R U Y Q M V (S) S

Write the circled letters here:

T E N N I S   B A L L S

Bats in the Belfry

Which one of these drawings is exactly the same as the ORIGINAL?
Look carefully and circle the one that is exactly the same.

ORIGINAL

① ② ③ ④ ⑤

Amoeboid

An amoeba is a really tiny, blobby-shaped creature. Only people with microscopes can see them. And the word amoeboid (UH-MEE-BOID) means "resembling an amoeba."

Your job is to write down as many words as possible using just the letters in AMOEBOID. No proper nouns and at least THREE letters long. OK, go!

9 WORDS — SMALLISH!

_____   _____   _____

_____   _____   _____

_____   _____   _____

18 WORDS — NOT AT ALL SMALLISH!!

_____   _____   _____

_____   _____   _____

_____   _____   _____

20 OR MORE — THE OPPOSITE OF SMALLISH!!!

_____   _____   _____

_____   _____   _____

Captain Overboard!

Use the clues to write one letter in each square. We did the first one to get you started. We also included the alphabet at the bottom to help with some of the clues. When you're done, read across to find the answer to this joke:

What does the pirate Bluebeard become when he falls in the Red Sea?

1. The letter before N
2. The 4th letter in BREAD
3. The letter that looks like a P, but with one additional line
4. The letter that looks the most like an egg
5. The letter that's in CLOAK but not LACK
6. The letter that looks like a Z turned on its side
7. The letter that's halfway between A and I
8. The middle letter in SCREWDRIVER

ABCDEFGHIJKLMNOPQRSTUVWXYZ

American History

There are seven questions on the left, and seven joke answers on the right.
Match them up by writing the correct number in each space.

Where was the Declaration of Independence signed?

A. ____

How were the first Americans like ants?

B. ____

Where did the pilgrims land when they came to America?

C. ____

Why does the Statue of Liberty stand in New York Harbor?

D. ____

What was worn at the Boston Tea Party?

E. ____

What did the cherry tree say after George Washington chopped it down?

F. ____

What was the most popular dance in 1776?

G. ____

1. On their feet.

2. I'm stumped.

3. At the bottom.

4. The Indepen-dance.

5. They lived in colonies.

6. T-shirts.

7. Because it can't sit down.

Bowing Bug

Put the 14 words into the grid in alphabetical order. We did the first one to get you started. Then write the highlighted letters from top to bottom in the spaces below to answer this joke:

What bug always gives thanks before eating?

FINAL

ALARM

LIMIT

NEIGH

PUMPS

RINSE

TITLE

MOUNT

UNITE

JOEYS

WASTE

CHAPS

DIARY

QUAIL

Write the highlighted letters here:

<u>A</u> _ _ _ _ _ _ _

_ _ _ _

A	L	A	R	M

At the Fair

Find and circle the 20 words listed below. The hidden words can read forward, backward, up, down, and diagonally in all directions.

```
S Y L M G B P N M W F J
A U L O J U T E K E P T
J I D L O M I H D T I B
X X V L V P J I E C H G
W O L I N E R N K M G O
D H L R A R O E K G E D
U K A H N C T D T E N T
E I D T O A V M R Z L O
N D O N B R S T A R E H
V D S X B Z Z R I J R L
O I X C I U L H N J A S
C E Z I R P W H E E L Y
```

JAM
PIE
LINE
LOOP

RIDE
SODA
TENT
PRIZE

THEME
TRAIN
WHEEL
WHIRL

HOT DOG
KIDDIE
RIBBON
THRILL

TICKET
PRETZEL
SNO-CONE
BUMPER CAR

Dribbling Allowed

Use the word and picture clues to
fill in the answers, one letter per square.

If you don't know an answer, try filling in ones
nearby or that go in the opposite direction.

1-Down

ACROSS

1 Body of water that's smaller than a sea but bigger than a lake
4 You ___ Here (phrase on a shopping mall map)
5 Hockey goalies wear them to protect their faces
7 Fluid in a pen
8 Had some food
9 Small child (it's a word that's spelled the same forward and backward)
12 Metal rod you grab to do chin-ups
13 Like a rowboat that's taking on water
15 Sick
16 Open from dawn '___ dusk

DOWN

1 It's dribbled on a court
2 Noah's boat in the Bible
3 The opposite of "no"
5 Girls name that's spelled with the letters in AIM
6 Little insect with tunnels in the ground and a hill for an entrance
10 Tree that makes acorns
11 Make an attempt
13 She ___ the candles on the cake (past tense of "light")
14 Cotton gin inventor Whitney or NFL quarterback Manning

5-Across

6-Down

7-Across

2-Down

Bloviate

loyal

Bloviate (BLOW-VEE-ATE) means to speak a lot and to use a lot of big words. Funny thing is, one who bloviates often doesn't have much worth saying!

Your job is to write down as many words as possible using just the letters in BLOVIATE. No proper nouns and at least THREE letters long. OK, go!

9 WORDS – YOU'RE PRETTY GOOD AT BLOVIATING!

bat	bit	bite
vat	lit	lot
late	lite	boat

18 WORDS – YOU'RE REALLY GOOD AT BLOVIATING!!

oat	tail	boil
bloat	bail	toil
vote	vail	ale

20 OR MORE – YOU ARE A SUPREME BLOVIATOR!!!

bale	bloviate	lab	bet
violate	tab	let	vet

Add 'Em Up

Here's a fun game for 2-4 players.

Players take turns. On each turn, draw one short line
that connects two dots. When a rectangle is completed,
surrounding a number, mark your initials on it.
The player who collects the most points wins!

Use both pages for one game or play two separate games.

Ben 74

Mom 52

1 1 1 1 1 1

2 2 2 2 2 2

1 1 1 1 1 1

4 4 4 4 4 4

1 1 1 1 1 1

6 6 9 9 1 1

1 1 9 9 1 1

6 6 6 6 6 6

1 1 1 1 1 1

4 4 4 4 4 4

1 1 1 1 1 1

2 2 2 2 2 2

Out of Africa

Cross off every letter that appears MORE THAN TWICE in the grid.
Then write the leftover letters (starting at the top and reading left to right)
in the spaces below to find the answer to this question:

**What is the capital
of Botswana?**

D C R W H J E Y M
F U G A V X K N S
P J Y O D S H G V
M N I X K W F Z U
Z V J E R O T V J
S A F D F N E H X
U R U Y G L K M Z
W M X K Z D O B V

Write the leftover letters here:

___ ___ ___ ___ ___ ___ ___ ___

Bike Cats

Which one of these drawings is exactly the same as the ORIGINAL?
Look carefully and circle the one that is exactly the same.

ORIGINAL

1

2

3

4

5

Fun at the Fair

There are 10 differences between the county fair scene on this page and the one on the next page. Can you find and circle all 10 of them?

Cool Ghoul

The answer to this joke is written using a simple code.

First, circle each letter that's immediately to the right of an X. We did the first one to get you started. Then write the circled letters (starting at the top and reading left to right) in the spaces below to answer this joke:

What do you get if you cross a snowman and a vampire?

I G C Z M X (F) E S M E V

E M I Q L J U K G S Z A

B U R X R U M R K Q O B

M F V R Q W I O R W K J

Z Q E N B O L X O B M I

B S M N I P X S D Q R K

A X T S L Z M G E D O Y

B M E E X B N R V I Z R

G F Z M R U Y Q M X I S

O Y Z G V M O U J B F W

A M N X T U N Z U M Y U

B Q N M T U X E V C E W

Write the circled letters here:

<u>F</u> _ _ _ _   _ _ _ _

Bufflehead

A bufflehead is a kind of diving duck with a big head.
A male bufflehead can puff out its head feathers to make it even bigger!

Your job is to write down as many words as possible using just the letters in BUFFLEHEAD No proper nouns and at least THREE letters long. OK, go!

9 WORDS — QUACKY!

18 WORDS — QUACKIER!!

20 OR MORE — QUACKIEST!!!

Clean Ocean

Use the clues to write one letter in each square. We did the first one to get you started. We also included the alphabet at the bottom to help with some of the clues. When you're done, read across to find the answer to this joke:

Who keeps the ocean floor tidy?

1. The letter that comes 2 letters before O
2. The letter that comes 6th in PRINCESS
3. The letter that's halfway between L and X
4. The letter that's repeated in MEMORY
5. The letter that's in both BALL and CHAIN
6. The letter that's a single straight line
7. The 4th letter of the alphabet
8. The letter that appears only once in TOOTS

ABCDEFGHIJKLMNOPQRSTUVWXYZ

Don't Blow It

Put the 10 words into the grid in alphabetical order. We did the first one to get you started. Then write the highlighted letters from top to bottom in the spaces below to answer this joke:

What kind of tests do balloons fear most?

PLAZA

APPLE

TRASH

KAPUT

LATIN

CLOCK

QUEEN

MAIZE

IRAQI

GUPPY

A	P	P	L	E

Write the highlighted letters here:

P __ __

__ __ __ __ __ __ __

A Phew Jokes

There are seven questions on the left, and seven joke answers on the right.
Match them up by writing the correct number in each space.

How do you stop a skunk from smelling?

A. 2

Why did the skunk bring toilet paper to the party?

B. 7

What did the judge say when a skunk came into the courtroom?

C. 1

Why are skunks smart?

D. 6

What do you get when you cross a bear and a skunk?

E. 3

What do all skunk jokes have in common?

F. 4

What do you call a flying skunk?

G. 5

1. Odor in the court.

2. Plug up its nose.

3. Winnie the P.U.

4. They stink.

5. A smell-icopter.

6. Because they have lots of scents.

7. Because it was a party pooper.

Birthday Time!

Find and circle the 20 words listed below. The hidden words can read forward, backward, up, down, and diagonally in all directions.

E L B A T J D G T J A I
Y T R A P J A C S O N T
D D A S N O O L L A B T
N V P T P N P J E O O E
A U O R Y I E W Z W W F
C W U E O K H R T I L N
A E T A L P A C E K A O
K X Q M D A T Z R R A C
E X A E E N S A P L U W
L D C R R P D R I N K S
L X U S R O V A F Z K C
L E K B S S E I K H A D

BOWL   SODA   OLDER   BANNER   BALLOONS
CAKE   CANDY   PARTY   DRINKS   CONFETTI
CUPS   CHIPS   PLATE   FAVORS   PRETZELS
HATS   CLOWN   TABLE   NAPKIN   STREAMERS

21

Furry Friend

Use the word and picture clues to fill in the answers, one letter per square.

If you don't know an answer, try filling in ones nearby or that go in the opposite direction.

1- Down →

ACROSS

1 Black, sticky road goo

~~**4** Dead~~ ___ (street that doesn't go through)

5 What shoulders, hips, and legs are part of

7 Fishing pole, or a boy's name

8 Use words that sound alike, as in poems

11 ___ constrictor (squeezing snake)

12 Not straight, such as a knee or elbow

13 The Mediterranean ___ (it's smaller than an ocean)

14 Letters added before "maid" to make it a woman with a fish tail

DOWN

1 Furry friend with stuffing for innards

2 "Are there ___ questions?"

3 Abbr. for "road" on a street sign

5 Sound made by someone who's shivering cold

6 ___ and aah (sounds made when watching fireworks)

9 Day before TUE on a calendar (abbr.)

10 Have breakfast, lunch, or dinner

12 Buzzing insect

13 Abbr. on a small T-shirt size

Crossword grid answers (handwritten):
Row 1: T E D D Y (with T, 2, 3 / E, N, D as TEND)
T
E N D
D
D
Y
B
E
A
R

1-Across

7- Across

Bzz Bzz Bzz

12-Down

9- Down

MARCH calendar

22

Doodle Mania

Find a path through this
crazy maze from Start to End.

Crudivore

This isn't pronounced like you may think. It's CROO-DA-VORE.
It means someone who eats only raw food.

Your job is to write down as many words as possible using just the letters in
CRUDIVORE. No proper nouns and at least THREE letters long. OK, go!

9 WORDS — REWARD YOURSELF WITH A RAW CARROT!

_____   _____   _____

_____   _____   _____

_____   _____   _____

18 WORDS — REWARD YOURSELF WITH TWO RAW CELERY STALKS!!

_____   _____   _____

_____   _____   _____

_____   _____   _____

20 OR MORE — REWARD YOURSELF WITH FIVE RAW ONIONS!!!

_____   _____   _____

_____   _____   _____

Copy Cat!

The answer to this joke is written using a simple code.

First, circle each letter that's immediately to the right of a C. We did the first one to get you started. Then write the circled letters (starting at the top and reading left to right) in the spaces below to answer this joke:

What is every cat in the world always doing at the same time?

I G W Z O H Q E S C Ⓖ X

C R I Q L J U K X S Z A

B J C O O U M R K Q O B

X M E E Q C W R V I Z R

G X Z M R U Y C I S K S

O Y C N V M O U J B F M

A M N I C G N Z U X Y U

V Q N M T U X C O W E J

M F V C L W I O R T K J

Z Q E N C D L P Z B M I

B S M N C E S R D Q R K

A C R S L Z M G E D O Y

Write the circled letters here:

<u>G</u> _ _ _ _ _ _ _   _ _ _ _ _

Fairy Smelly

Use the clues to write one letter in each square. We did the first one to get you started. We also included the alphabet at the bottom to help with some of the clues. When you're done, read across to find the answer to this joke:

What do you call a fairy who won't take a bath?

The first word:

1. The letter that comes after R
2. The letter in TOSS-UP that's made with only straight lines
3. The letter that sounds like a body part you see with
4. The middle letter in THUNDER
5. The letter repeated in KENTUCKY
6. The letter missing in ABCDF
7. The letter that comes 5 letters after M

The second word:

8. The letter that's in both BIRD and BEE
9. The middle letter in SHELL
10. The letter between K and M
11. The letter halfway between H and P

1	2	3	4	5	6	7
S						

8	9	10	11

No thanks!

ABCDEFGHIJKLMNOPQRSTUVWXYZ

Gobbling

Put the 11 words into the grid in alphabetical order. We did the first one to get you started. Then write the highlighted letters from top to bottom in the spaces below to answer this joke:

What are turkeys thankful for on Thanksgiving?

CHESS

NORTH

ZESTY

FRESH

ANVIL

MEANT

EAGLE

TRADE

QUIET

WINCE

KITES

A	N	V	I	L
C	H	E	S	S
E	A	G	L	E
F	R	E	S	h
K	I	T	E	s
M	E	A	N	T
N	O	R	T	h
Q	U	I	E	t
T	r	a	d	e
W	I	N	C	E
Z	E	S	T	Y

Thank you!

Write the highlighted letters here: <u>V</u> <u>E</u> <u>G</u> <u>E</u> <u>T</u> <u>A</u> <u>R</u> <u>I</u> <u>A</u> <u>N</u> <u>S</u>

Boat-igator

Which one of these drawings is exactly the same as the ORIGINAL?
Look carefully and circle the one that is exactly the same.

ORIGINAL

①

②

③

④

⑤

Critters

Find and circle the 20 words listed below. The hidden words can read forward, backward, up, down, and diagonally in all directions.

M O O S E B Q H E D R N
Q O S U I Q E K R U H M
D R N T I B B A R A U A
I R A K B Q Z C R K C R
E M K W E I K L D M J M
L S E F L Y R X U B M Y
A K R L E C E D H X G I
H U J O P I G C P T O C
W N B W H N O O C C A R
Q K O C A T D E E R T P
I F T I N S E C T D X S
K R E J T U R T L E L J

 CAT  BIRD  HORSE WHALE RABBIT
DOG DEER MOOSE INSECT TURTLE
PIG GOAT SKUNK LIZARD RACCOON
BEAR WOLF SNAKE MONKEY ELEPHANT

29

Birthdays!

There are seven questions on the left, and seven joke answers on the right.
Match them up by writing the correct number in each space.

What do Columbus and Lincoln have in common?

A. ____

What goes up but never comes down?

B. ____

What do they serve at birthday parties in heaven?

C. ____

What do cats like to eat on their birthdays?

D. ____

What do you call a birthday present the day after you get it?

E. ____

Why are birthdays good for your health?

F. ____

Why do we put candles on top of a birthday cake?

G. ____

1. A birthday past.

2. The more you have, the longer you live.

3. It's hard to put them on the bottom.

4. Your age.

5. Cake and mice cream.

6. They were both born on holidays.

7. Angel food cake.

Going in Reverse

Use the word and picture clues to
fill in the answers, one letter per square.

If you don't know an answer, try filling in ones
nearby or that go in the opposite direction.

ACROSS

1 Not against (such as supporters of the home team)
4 What a basketball net is attached to
7 10 - 8 = ___
8 Girl's name (it's spelled the same forward and backward)
9 Piles of pancakes
11 Drink that's a lot like beer
12 "I didn't ___ (see) anything odd"
15 Two words said when getting married
16 Amaze
18 Word that means "for each," as in: Only one soda ___ person
19 Strawberry or tomato color

DOWN

1 Abbreviation for foot or fort
2 "Ouch, that hurts!" sounds
3 Spinning thing (it's spelled the same forward and backward)
4 Fast vehicle (it's spelled the same forward and backward; 2 words)
5 Black stuff squirted by an octopus
6 Mothers, for short
10 Aladdin hero
12 Small bite made by a puppy
13 Type of poem
14 Female sheep (it's spelled the same forward and backward)
17 Nickname for Edward

9-Across

19-Across

4-Down

17

Don't Move!

Cross off every letter that appears MORE THAN TWICE in the grid.
Then write the leftover letters (starting at the top and reading left to right)
in the spaces below to find the answer to this question:

**What goes up and down and yet
always stays in the same place?**

S B P J U K N C G
L T V H W D Y M X
U N F B K Z J C O
E V X A L M H K F
E P H Z D I Y W J
M P F B U V X N Z
C O K Z G W Y R E
L H O G D U M L S

Write the leftover letters here:

— — — — — —

Chickens' Day Out

Take a minute or two to study this drawing. Try to remember everything in it. Then turn the page and see how well you do at answering the 10 questions about it.

WAIT!

Don't read any further if you haven't looked at the page BEFORE this one.

Chickens' Day Out

OK, now let's see what you remember.

Write your answers in the blanks after each question.

1. How many chickens are at the table? _____

2. Name one of the foods on the table. Name a second for extra credit.

   _____

3. What is the name written on the side of the rowboat?

   _____

4. How many bushes with red berries are there? _____

5. How many chickens are jogging on the trail up top? _____

6. Are the two chickens in the boat wearing hats? YES or NO_____

7. How many animals are wearing sunglasses? _____

8. How many cats are in the picture? _____

9. How many chickens are in the water (not in a boat)? _____

10. What word is on the wire basket in the upper left? _____

Dots the Way

There are many ways to get from Start to End. But only one route visits just SEVEN red dots. The other routes visit more. Can you find it?

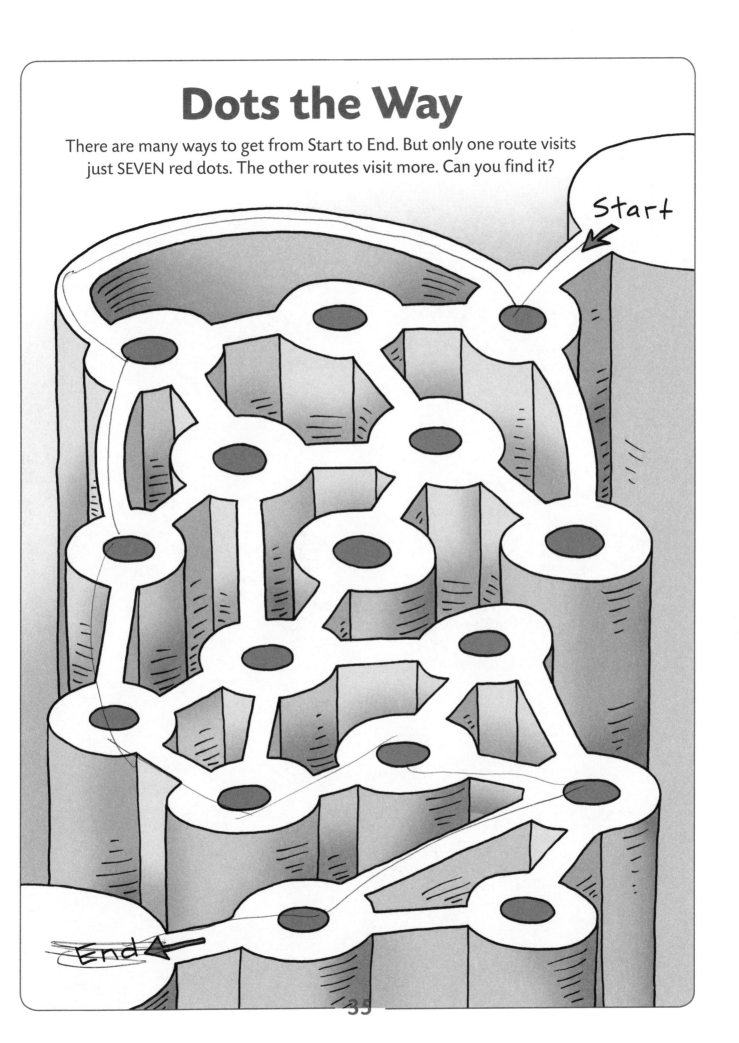

Clowning Around

Which one of these drawings is exactly the same as the ORIGINAL?
Look carefully and circle the one that is exactly the same.

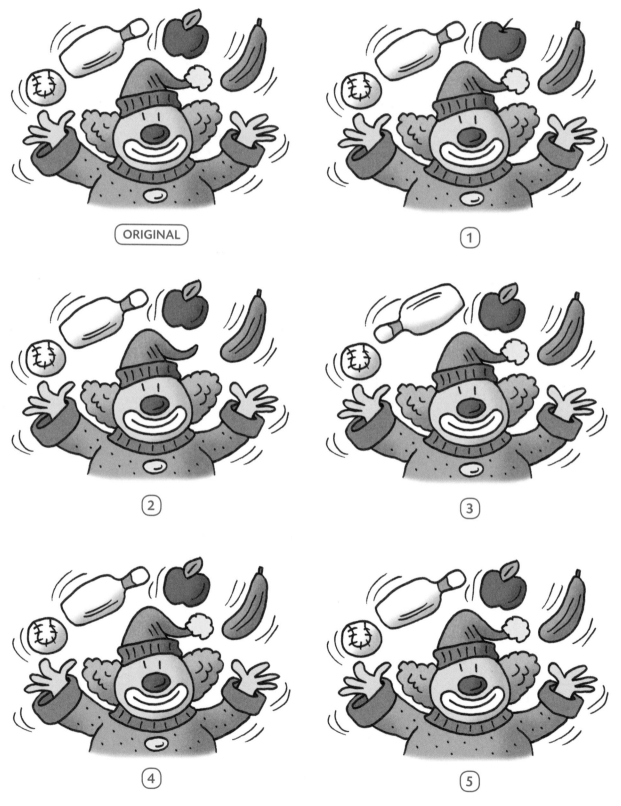

ORIGINAL

1

2

3

4

5

Feed the Kitty

Use five coins to feed all nine cats!

Shake the coins in your hands, then drop them. If there is one heads (four tails), mark your initials on the belly of a cat that's holding up a 1. If there are two heads (three tails), initial the belly of a cat holding a 2, and so on. Initial no bellies if you toss either zero or five heads, or if you have already finished off the number tossed.

Take turns if you play with a friend.
First to feed all nine cats wins!

Dish Is Funny

The answer to this joke is written using a simple code.

First, circle each letter that's immediately to the right of a P. We did the first one to get you started. Then write the circled letters (starting at the top and reading left to right) in the spaces below to answer this joke:

What did the one plate say to the other?

P Ⓓ E F Q E N R V I Z R

G X P I R U Y Q M S K S

R Y Z G V P N U J B F W

L M N I Q U N Z U X P N

P E N M T U X O V C E W

I G C P R H Q E S M E X

Z Q E N B O P I Z B M I

T S M N P S S R I Q R K

A U Q P O Z M G E F O Y

E M I Q L J P N X S Z A

G U X M O U M R K P M B

M F V P E W I O R W K J

Write the circled letters here:

D _ _ _ _ _ _ _   _ _   _ _   _ _

Folderol

Folderol (FALL-DE-RALL) is nonsense or a lot of silly
fuss made about something that's total nonsense.

Your job is to write down as many words as possible using just the letters
in FOLDEROL. No proper nouns and at least THREE letters long. OK, go!

9 WORDS — SILLY!

_____ _____ _____

_____ _____ _____

_____ _____ _____

18 WORDS — SILLIER!!

_____ _____ _____

_____ _____ _____

_____ _____ _____

20 OR MORE — SILLIEST YET!!!

_____ _____ _____

_____ _____ _____

Filling His Sack

Use the clues to write one letter in each square. We did the first one to get you started. We also included the alphabet at the bottom to help with some of the clues. When you're done, read across to find the answer to this joke:

Where does Santa go to buy potatoes?

1. The letter before J
2. The letter that's just a little better grade than an F
3. The 2nd, 4th, and 6th letter in PAJAMAS
4. The middle letter of MACHINE
5. The vowel that comes 4th in the alphabet
6. The letter that's in REACH but not RACE
7. The letter between N and P
8. The 7th letter of STRETCHED
9. The letter that comes 12 letters after C

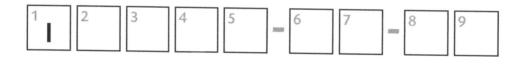

ABCDEFGHIJKLMNOPQRSTUVWXYZ

I'm Not Moving!

Put the 12 words into the grid in alphabetical order. We did the first one to get you started. Then write the highlighted letters from top to bottom in the spaces below to answer this joke:

What has two legs but can't walk?

YEAST

MUMPS

AMAZE

BUMPS

HOOEY

TEETH

FRAIL

GUARD

DREAM

LIFTS

NAVAL

OWING

Write the highlighted letters here:

<u>A</u> _ _ _ _

_ _ _ _ _

A	M	A	Z	E

Gimme Some Space

There are seven questions on the left, and seven joke answers on the right.
Match them up by writing the correct number in each space.

What is an astronaut's favorite part of a computer keyboard?

A. ____

What did the alien cat say when it landed on Earth?

B. ____

Where did the cow go after jumping over the moon?

C. ____

Why is Saturn rich?

D. ____

How do you know when the moon is going broke?

E. ____

If an athlete gets athlete's foot what does an astronaut get?

F. ____

How do you get a baby to sleep in space?

G. ____

1. Mistletoe (missile toe).

2. Because it has lots of rings.

3. Rocket (rock it) to sleep.

4. Take me to your litter.

5. The space bar.

6. The Milky Way.

7. When it's down to its last quarter.

Flower Power

Find and circle the 20 words listed below. The hidden words can read forward, backward, up, down, and diagonally in all directions.

G A R D E N I A V D D T
Y Z C A R N A T I O N L L
N A W F C M T H O R N V
O L C F O A C Q T U I V
E E S O R R T U S V P S
P A L D O I C U L C C V
A B A I O G C D L M G Z
N R T L T O N A T I O D
S T E M R L N H L Z P M
Y D P C M D B L D I H W
S E V B O D A I S Y L Q
L I X S W H G A S G I K

IRIS
ROOT
ROSE
STEM

BLOOM
DAISY
LILAC
PANSY

PEONY
PETAL
THORN
TULIP

AZALEA
CROCUS
DAHLIA
ORCHID

DAFFODIL
GARDENIA
MARIGOLD
CARNATION

43

Happy Times

Use the word and picture clues to
fill in the answers, one letter per square.

If you don't know an answer, try filling in ones
nearby or that go in the opposite direction.

1-Down

ACROSS

1 The opposite of "good"
4 Cold cubes in the freezer
5 Witch's ___ (boiling mixture in a big pot)
6 Small house with bamboo walls and a palm tree roof
7 Gray leftover stuff in a fireplace
10 Little circle on top of an i or a j
11 Beautiful, white long-necked water bird
13 Give money when buying something
14 They're gained during a football game (abbr.)

DOWN

1 Once-a-year occasions with presents and cake
2 The highest card in a deck of cards
3 Little drops of water covering the grass early in the morning
5 Yellow vehicle for getting many kids to and from school
6 Laughed-out-loud word
8 Very long period of time
9 Abbr. following Main or Elm on a street sign
11 Secret agent
12 Gob of gum

(grid answers filled in: 1 B A D, 4 I C E, 5 B R E W, 6 H U T, 7 A S H E S, 10 O, 11 S W A N, 13 P A Y, 14 D S)

Main st.

4-Across

11-Across

2-Down

6-Across

5-Down

SCHOOL

44

Hop To It

Following the arrows, find the one path that
visits each and every lily pad exactly once.

Start

End

Gasconade

Gasconade (GAS-CON-ADE) isn't some kind of fruity drink. It's just another word for boasting, such as: "His speech was filled with gasconade." Know anyone like that?

Your job is to write down as many words as possible using just the letters in GASCONADE. No proper nouns and at least THREE letters long. OK, go!

9 WORDS — WORTH BRAGGING ABOUT A LITTLE!

_____   _____   _____

_____   _____   _____

_____   _____   _____

18 WORDS — WORTH BRAGGING ABOUT A LOT!!

_____   _____   _____

_____   _____   _____

_____   _____   _____

20 OR MORE — BRAG ALL YOU WANT!!!

_____   _____   _____

_____   _____   _____

Don't Coat Me On This

The answer to this joke is written using a simple code.

First, circle each letter that's immediately to the right of a W. We did the first one to get you started. Then write the circled letters (starting at the top and reading left to right) in the spaces below to answer this joke:

What coat is always wet when you put it on?

R M Z G V M O T J W Ⓐ B

W Ⓒ N I Q U N Z U X Y U

B Q W Ⓞ T U X O V E E E

I G B W Ⓐ H Q E S M E X

K M I Q L J W Ⓣ X S Z A

Z Q E N B W Ⓞ P Z B M I

X M W Ⓕ Q E N R V I Z R

W Ⓟ Z M R U Y Q M S K S

B U X D O U M R K Q W Ⓐ

J F V R Q L I O W Ⓘ K J

B S W Ⓝ I X S R D Q R K

W Ⓣ Q S L Z M G E D O Y

Write the circled letters here:

A COAT OF PAINT

47

Dog and Fox Trot

Which one of these drawings is exactly the same as the ORIGINAL?
Look carefully and circle the one that is exactly the same.

ORIGINAL

1

2

3

4

5

Frank Firster

Use the clues to write one letter in each square. We did the first one to get you started. We also included the alphabet at the bottom to help with some of the clues. When you're done, read across to find the answer to this joke:

What did the hot dog say when it won the race?

The first word:

1. The letter that's another word for ME
2. The repeated letter in MUMMY

The second word:

3. The middle letter of SIGNATURE

The third word:

4. The letter that looks like an upside-down M
5. The letter between H and J
6. The 1st letter when you spell out the number 8
7. The letter that's in both SONG and DANCE
8. The 5th letter of the alphabet
9. The 6th letter of UNIVERSE

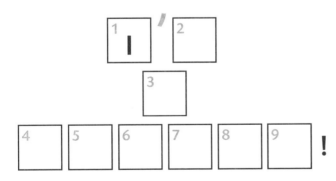

ABCDEFGHIJKLMNOPQRSTUVWXYZ

Food's On!

Find and circle the 20 words listed below. The hidden words can read forward, backward, up, down, and diagonally in all directions.

```
M J Y E W J J H A P K U
G Y N E K C I H C A H S
N O C A B S G G E N B E
U I O T A M O T R C U I
R M F R I E S O E A R L
C C H L T J A A A K G G
B T K E U Q N S L E E G
G R E N N I D T V S R B
I O V S A H W Y D A R P
U L O F R U I T V L P V
U L O T Q S C Y J A I U
N S T W V N H P R D X B
```

EGGS	BACON	LUNCH	TOAST	TOMATO
MILK	FRIES	ROLLS	BURGER	CHICKEN
RICE	FRUIT	SALAD	CEREAL	PANCAKES
TUNA	GRAVY	STEAK	DINNER	SANDWICH

In Apple Pie Order

There are seven questions on the left, and seven joke answers on the right.
Match them up by writing the correct number in each space.

What did the apple say to the orange? A. ____

Who led the apples to the bakery? B. ____

When is an apple grouchy? C. ____

If an apple a day keeps the doctor away, what does an onion do? D. ____

What kind of fruit do you get if you cross Christmas trees with apple trees? E. ____

What's the best thing to put into an apple pie? F. ____

What do you call apples with bees in front of them? G. ____

1. Keeps everyone away.

2. Pineapples.

3. The pie piper.

4. Nothing, apples can't talk.

5. Your teeth.

6. Bapples.

7. When it's a crab apple.

Loco Motive

Put the 14 words into the grid in alphabetical order. We did the first one to get you started. Then write the highlighted letters from top to bottom in the spaces below to answer this joke:

How does a train eat?

RHYME

CRATE

DIGIT

HATCH

OCEAN

MEOWS

ITCHY

GUSTY

FIEND

BRAIN

SERVE

TWIST

EVOKE

LEVEL

Write the highlighted letters here:

I _ _   _ _ _ _ _

_ _ _ _   _ _ _ _

B	R	A	I	N

Kick Ball

Cross off every letter that appears MORE THAN TWICE in the grid.
Then write the leftover letters (starting at the top and reading left to right)
in the spaces below to find the answer to this question:

**What direction should you kick a ball
if you want to easily get it back?**

V N B O S C J D M

E K W T B R L X F

Z V Y D A N O W Z

M J I B X C G L E

K F V Y H F D J Z

Y T X K C M W O E

N M Z U F B Y J E

O W V D X N P C L

Write the leftover letters here:

__ __ __ __ __ __ __ __ __ __

Elf Portrait

Which one of these drawings is exactly the same as the ORIGINAL?
Look carefully and circle the one that is exactly the same.

ORIGINAL

①

②

③

④

⑤

Fang You Very Much

The answer to this joke is written using a simple code.

First, circle each letter that's immediately to the right of an F. We did the first one to get you started. Then write the circled letters (starting at the top and reading left to right) in the spaces below to answer this joke:

What part of the street do vampires live on?

T R X D F (T) V E N R Q W

P H R W K J F H Y V N G

E O U J F E W V N N I Q

U N Z U X Y U B Q N V I

U D O B C F D I G C Z E

H Q E F E E M E M A Q L

J F A X S Z A Q W A S Y

Z Q E N V B L P F D M I

B S M N I X S R D Q V A

V L Q S L Z F E E D O Y

X F N V L E N R P I Z R

G X Z M R U Y Q M V F D

Write the circled letters here:

T _ _ _ _ _ _ _ _ _

Hyperbole

Hyperbole (HI-PER-BOWL-EE) is exaggerated talk, such as saying, "That ice cream cone is a mile high and the best one in the entire world!"

Your job is to write down as many words as possible using just the letters in HYPERBOLE. No proper nouns and at least THREE letters long. OK, go!

9 WORDS — THE BEST WORDS EVER!

_____   _____   _____

_____   _____   _____

_____   _____   _____

18 WORDS — NO, WAIT, THESE ARE EVEN BETTER!!

_____   _____   _____

_____   _____   _____

_____   _____   _____

20 OR MORE — AND YET YOU'VE FOUND SOME THAT ARE EVEN GREATER!!!

_____   _____   _____

_____   _____   _____

In the Neighborhood

Find and circle the 20 words listed below. The hidden words can read forward, backward, up, down, and diagonally in all directions.

```
X S E W E R E B N C S E
S J C Y O C Z V X R G S
E X L A N E Q C B C P M
S I D E W A L K V U I P
U L F N G D E H S R S F
O Q H M C A M N S B T H
H J L X B S R W A X O N
W H B D C T K A R A O A
T Q J L U M J L G C P Y
B G K K O Y E L L A A Y
E P Q M K C T E E R T S
C P S B G M K I D S H E
```

CAR	KIDS	SHED	FENCE	STOOP
BUSH	LAWN	YARD	GRASS	GARAGE
CURB	PATH	ALLEY	HOUSE	STREET
GATE	ROAD	BLOCK	SEWER	SIDEWALK

Let's Be Frank

Cross off every letter that appears MORE THAN TWICE in the grid.
Then write the leftover letters (starting at the top and reading left to right)
in the spaces below to find the answer to this question:

**How do you make
a hot dog stand?**

Z S B W F U G P K

Y D T N V J E M O

X K M A O Z B J L

V U X G I F P N P

J T Y W K D S X W

N G C O M U G V P

H Z D N B F Y A J

M J I O K U R X Z

Write the leftover letters here:

_ _ _ _ _ _ _   _ _ _ _ _   _ _ _ _ _

Fruit Feet

Use the clues to write one letter in each square. We did the first one to get you started. We also included the alphabet at the bottom to help with some of the clues. When you're done, read across to find the answer to this joke:

Who makes shoes for fruit?

The first word:

1. The letter that comes after O
2. The letter that has three straight lines pointing to the right
3. The letter that's farthest from Z
4. The letter that sounds like SEA
5. The letter that starts with an A sound (but it's not the letter A)

The second word:

6. The middle letter of APPLICATION
7. The most common letter in FOOTNOTE
8. The letter that comes 10 letters before L
9. The letter that comes 9 letters before K
10. The 5th letter in FAMILY
11. The letter that's repeated in EAGLE
12. The letter that isn't repeated in STREETS
13. The last letter of most plural words

ABCDEFGHIJKLMNOPQRSTUVWXYZ

May the Sweets Be With You

Put the 10 words into the grid in alphabetical order. We did the first one to get you started. Then write the highlighted letters from top to bottom in the spaces below to answer this joke:

What is a Jedi Knight's favorite candy?

WHEEL

SCRAM

EMAIL

CLAIM

MUFFS

PRISM

DEALT

OCTET

YEARN

VALVE

C	L	A	I	M

Interstellar Candy Store

open

Write the highlighted letters here:

<u>A</u>

_ _ _ _ _ _ _ _ _ _ _

Mr. Puss

Starting at Mr. Puss, follow the different pieces of yarn
to find out which one leads to the yarn ball.

End

Start

1
2
3 4 5

NO

NO

NO NO

I Spy

Use the word and picture clues to
fill in the answers, one letter per square.

If you don't know an answer, try filling in ones
nearby or that go in the opposite direction.

3-
Down

ACROSS

1 ___ Vegas, Nevada
4 How old you are
is your ___
5 Bugs Bunny line:
"What's up, ___?"
(also a short word for
a medical person)
6 Word in a
cheerleader's cheer
9 What you see with
10 "And they lived
happily ever ___"
12 Vegetable used to
make a thick green
soup
13 Type of leg for a
pirate (it's wooden)
14 What you hear with
17 Pen point
18 Letters added in front
of "cycle" that makes
it a three-wheeler

DOWN

1 Young boy
2 "How long ___ did
you get here?"
3 Undercover spy
(2 words)
7 "Yes," aboard a
pirate ship
8 Opposite of "him"
10 A 99¢ game added
on to a smartphone,
for example
11 Admission price, or
a doctor's charge
15 The stuff you
breathe
16 Baseball abbreviation
for "runs batted in"

12
Across

6-Across!

18-
Across

Looking for a Lake

Cross off every letter that appears MORE THAN TWICE in the grid.
Then write the leftover letters (starting at the top and reading left to right)
in the spaces below to find the answer to this question:

**What state is
Lake Tahoe in?**

R B N W L G T H V

J S F Z V C K X S

Y E G R I M B H Z

A X N Q J W T F

M Z H E S K V Y C

P B F A U R W P T

C A G Y I X J H M

V P Z B D P K R E

Write the leftover letters here:

— — — — — —

Having a Beach Ball

Which one of these drawings is exactly the same as the ORIGINAL?
Look carefully and circle the one that is exactly the same.

ORIGINAL

①

②

③

④

⑤

Outstanding in His Field

Use the clues to write one letter in each square. We did the first one to get you started. We also included the alphabet at the bottom to help with some of the clues. When you're done, read across to find the answer to this joke:

What did Baby Corn ask Mom Corn?

The first word:

1. The letter before X
2. The letter between G and I
3. The letter that's repeated in EEK
4. The letter that sounds like the verb in YOU ARE HERE
5. The most common letter in TEMPERATURE

The second word:

6. The middle letter of CAPITAL
7. The beginning or end of SNAKES

The third word:

8. The letter that sounds like a little, round, green vegetable
9. The letter that sounds like OH
10. The letter that's repeated in PURPLE
11. The letter that appears once in ONCE but never in ONE
12. The letter that appears in DOUBLE or NOTHING
13. The letter that's 5 letters before the T in RABBIT
14. The middle letter of EXPLANATION

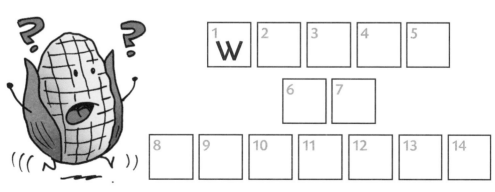

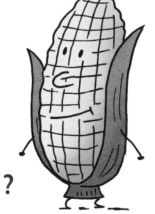

ABCDEFGHIJKLMNOPQRSTUVWXYZ

Stationary Bike

Cross off every letter that appears MORE THAN TWICE in the grid.
Then write the leftover letters (starting at the top and reading left to right)
in the spaces below to find the answer to this question:

Why wouldn't the
bike go any farther?

A X H V C Y T K P

M S G W Z H L C U

B Y P K A O X F M

U T X N V S P H Z

L F I M B A U K G

B R S Z Y L C F P

N V G M E S Y H U

C N K F V D A B M

Write the leftover letters here:

IT WAS ___ ___ ___   ___ ___ ___ ___

Monster Mash

Take a minute or two to study this drawing. Try to remember everything in it. Then turn the page and see how well you do at answering the 10 questions about it.

WAIT!

Don't read any further if you haven't
looked at the page BEFORE this one.

Monster Mash

OK, now let's see what you remember.

Write your answers in the blanks
after each question.

1. How many ghosts are there in the wooden tub? _____

2. What is the name of the big, purple, globby monster? _____

3. There's a green octopus-like tentacle in the upper left. What is it doing?

_____

4. Are any of the monsters wearing hats? YES or NO _____

5. What is the vat number on the wooden tub? _____

6. What is the number of snakes listed on the sign on the side of the crate? _____

7. How many snakes can you see IN the crate? _____

8. How many snakes can you see OUTSIDE the crate? _____

9. What is the crocodile in the lower right doing? _____

10. What kind of cereal is in the box? _____

La La Land

There are seven questions on the left, and seven joke answers on the right.
Match them up by writing the correct number in each space.

Why wouldn't the piano play any music?

A. ____

What makes music on your hair?

B. ____

Why are pirates great singers?

C. ____

What rock group has four guys who don't sing?

D. ____

What is a cat's favorite song?

E. ____

What has forty feet and sings?

F. ____

What is a vampire's favorite part of the guitar?

G. ____

LA LA LA LA LA LA LA

1. A Head Band.

2. Mount Rushmore.

3. It lost its keys.

4. A school choir.

5. The neck.

6. Three Blind Mice.

7. They're always hitting the high C's.

It's Magic!

Find and circle the 20 words listed below. The hidden words can read forward, backward, up, down, and diagonally in all directions.

```
S F Q X T D Q N M D N T
F F D N J P W R F N Z R O
C C L I W B L T A L E O Z
B B H L A T E W B G D C F
F F C B R M P F L S O I C
A A T O S O R C E R Y N S
F F I G Z O E E L F S U P
W W B G R C Y M L A O R I
E E A S N K H A R Y T I T
E E R G O J A Q X I N B T
H H T E M P U S O N A P E
Y Y S K E S N N V G F F B
```

 ELF
FROG
OGRE
TALE

 WAND
FABLE
FAIRY
GNOME

 WARTS
WITCH
DRAGON
FLYING

 GOBLIN
POTION
SPRITE
FANTASY

 MERMAID
SORCERY
UNICORN
LEPRECHAUN

Polar Exploration

Which penguin chick belongs to which parent?
Follow the tangled lines to find out. Then write the
correct letter on the line below the parent's number.

X Marks the Spot

Use the word and picture clues to
fill in the answers, one letter per square.

If you don't know an answer, try filling in ones
nearby or that go in the opposite direction.

1-Down

ACROSS

1 2,000 pounds
4 Stroke, as a dog's belly
5 Period of history (when spelled backwards, it's the plural of "is")
6 Salty body of water
8 Sounds people make when they get hurt
9 Dr. ___ (author of *The Cat in the Hat*)
12 Style of music that's features a strong beat and spoken rhyme
13 Abbr. for "expected time of arrival," such as when a flight is due
14 Short word for mother
16 Word of discovery when cracking a case
17 Smallish spoon measurement (abbr.)

DOWN

1 Paper marked with an X to show where a valuable chest is buried (2 words)
2 "It'll be ___ secret" (yours and my)
3 Org. for basketball teams like the Knicks and the Lakers (abbreviation)
6 Letters meaning "help!" when a ship is sinking
7 Female sheep
10 Used a chair or bench
11 Relaxing place to go (maybe even get a mud bath)
14 "Welcome" might be printed on it below the front door
15 Surprised sounds

1-Across

7-Down

14-Down

Welcome

On the Road

Fill in the boxes in the BLANK GRID by copying exactly what you see in the same-numbered boxes in the SCRAMBLED GRID.

SCRAMBLED GRID

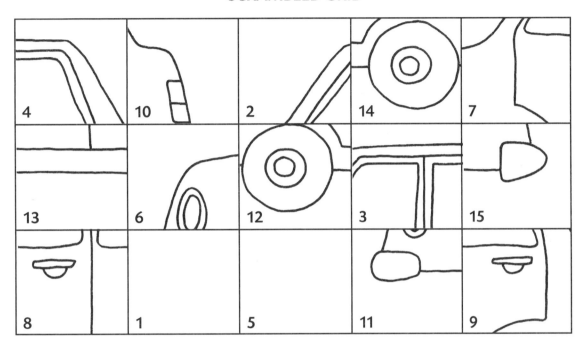

BLANK GRID

Low   High

Jokesmith

A smith is someone who makes something.
So a jokesmith is someone who makes jokes. Simple, right?

Your job is to write down as many words as possible using just the letters in JOKESMITH. No proper nouns and at least THREE letters long. OK, go!

9 WORDS – GREAT!

_____   _____   _____

_____   _____   _____

_____   _____   _____

18 WORDS – GREATER!!

_____   _____   _____

_____   _____   _____

_____   _____   _____

20 OR MORE – GREATEST!!!

_____   _____   _____

_____   _____   _____

On the Beach

Find and circle the 20 words listed below. The hidden words can read forward, backward, up, down, and diagonally in all directions.

```
Z Q O M R F Q Q H W K K
H B O A R D W A L K L W
U Z G S H O V E L I Y G
C G F P L F P W A T E R
W O O X I E B P B D U U
A H A T H E A H H F M P
V D Z S H A R K C R B Z
E D I T T Q C H A I R E
S U N G L A S S E S E F
K N B L U L U I B B L R
L E W O T L U F W E L P
X S A N D I L Q J E A B
```

CRAB
FISH
GULL
PAIL

PIER
SAND
TIDE
CHAIR

COAST
DUNES
SHARK
TOWEL

WATER
WAVES
SHOVEL
FRISBEE

UMBRELLA
BEACHBALL
BOARDWALK
SUNGLASSES

On the Moon

Which one of these drawings is exactly the same as the ORIGINAL?
Look carefully and circle the one that is exactly the same.

ORIGINAL

①

②

③

④

⑤

Science...Not!

Use the clues to write one letter in each square. We did the first one to get you started. We also included the alphabet at the bottom to help with some of the clues. When you're done, read across to find the answer to this joke:

How do you make antifreeze?

The first word:

1. The 1st letter in SCIENCE
2. The letter that sounds like a little peg you put a golfball on
3. The most common letter in ENVELOPE
4. The middle letter in OPERATION
5. The 12th letter of the alphabet

The second word:

6. The last letter in TRASH
7. The vowel that's repeated in LETTER
8. The letter that's 4 letters after N

The third word:

9. The most common letter in BUBBLEGUM
10. The letter that looks like the left side and bottom of a rectangle
11. The 7th letter of INFORMATION
12. The letter that's in NOW and AGAIN
13. The letter that's in TRUNK but not RUNT
14. The 2nd vowel alphabetically
15. The letter that starts TROUBLE

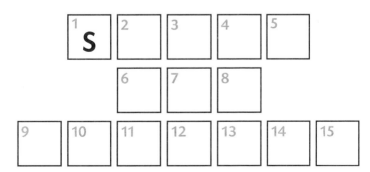

ABCDEFGHIJKLMNOPQRSTUVWXYZ

Show Me the Money

There are seven questions on the left, and seven joke answers on the right.
Match them up by writing the correct number in each space.

Where do fish keep their money?

A. ____

How do dinosaurs pay their bills?

B. ____

Why did the crook shower before robbing a bank?

C. ____

What has two heads and two tails but no arms or legs?

D. ____

What kind of money do crabs use?

E. ____

Why is a football game worth a dollar?

F. ____

Why is a nickel smarter than a penny?

G. ____

1. Sand dollars.

2. Two pennies.

3. With Tyrannosaurus checks.

4. It has more cents.

5. He wanted to make a clean getaway.

6. In river banks.

7. It has four quarters.

On the Farm

Find and circle the 20 words listed below. The hidden words can read forward, backward, up, down, and diagonally in all directions.

```
M U J F V G X A P Y H X
A G T N Z Z N E P A G T
W B A R N E K C I H C D
S I L O N I A R G O X F
W O R C E R A C S W O C
D O Z P D T M E H O R E
B G L F D R L A E B C K
B O F P K A T D E B H V
H D O K B C E F P M A D
G E M M F T W R O N R K
N A A Q J O F I E L D M
O G U H O R S E E D S U
```

HAY   COWS   SILO   GRAIN   CHICKEN
PEN   LOFT   VANE   HORSE   ORCHARD
BARN   PIGS   BALES   SEEDS   TRACTOR
CORN   PLOW   FIELD   SHEEP   SCARECROW

Stay Awake!

Cross off every letter that appears MORE THAN TWICE in the grid.
Then write the leftover letters (starting at the top and reading left to right)
in the spaces below to find the answer to this question:

**How can you go eight
days without sleep?**

B S V C W D Q J R

K Y F X L E K M U

Z R E B V C F Z P

U A Q J W M B D X

K R F T X Y C U W

D B N M J U I Q Z

C X B G K V R W F

M Q Y J H V D Z T

Write the leftover letters here:

_ _ _ _ _   _ _   _ _ _ _ _

Termite Time

The answer to this joke is written using a simple code.

First, circle each letter that's immediately to the right of a D. We did the first one to get you started. Then write the circled letters (starting at the top and reading left to right) in the spaces below to answer this joke:

What do termites eat for dessert?

R Q D (T) T U X O V C E W

I G C Z M H Q E S M E X

E M I Q L D O K X S Z A

D O X P O U M R K Q O B

G F D T Q W I O R W K J

Z Q E N B O L P Z B M I

B S M N I X D H F Q R K

A D P S L Z M G E C O Y

L M E E Q E N R V I D I

G X Z M R D C Q M S K S

O Y D K V M O U J B F W

A M N I Q U N Z U D S U

Write the circled letters here:

<u>T</u> _ _ _ _ _ _ _ _ _

81

Petty Party

Which one of these drawings is exactly the same as the ORIGINAL?
Look carefully and circle the one that is exactly the same.

ORIGINAL

1

2

3

4

5

Peabrain

Peabrain is what you might call someone who isn't too smart. But you're a very polite person — we can tell — so it's unlikely you've ever used such a word.

Your job is to write down as many words as possible using just the letters in PEABRAIN. No proper nouns and at least THREE letters long. OK, go!

9 WORDS – YOU'RE NO PEABRAIN!

_____   _____   _____

_____   _____   _____

_____   _____   _____

18 WORDS – YOU'RE REALLY NOT A PEABRAIN!!

_____   _____   _____

_____   _____   _____

_____   _____   _____

20 OR MORE – YOU'RE THE UN-PEABRAINIEST!!!

_____   _____   _____

_____   _____   _____

Sick as a Dog

Use the clues to write one letter in each square. We did the first one to get you started. We also included the alphabet at the bottom to help with some of the clues. When you're done, read across to find the answer to this joke:

What does a sick dog say?

The first word:

1. The 2nd letter of the alphabet
2. The letter made by adding a line to an upside-down V
3. The middle letter of AMPERSAND (that's the word for this: &)
4. The most common letter in OFFICE

The second word:

5. The letter that sounds like a buzzing insect
6. The letter that's repeated in ALPHABET
7. The letter that sounds like the verb ARE
8. The 6th letter of the alphabet

The third word:

9. The middle letter in the word PROBLEM
10. The letter that comes nine letters before J
11. The letter between Q and S
12. The letter that appears in both FORE and AFT

1 B	2	3	4
5	6	7	8
9	10	11	12

FIDO

ABCDEFGHIJKLMNOPQRSTUVWXYZ

Monster Match

Put the 14 words into the grid in alphabetical order. We did the first one to get you started. Then write the highlighted letters from top to bottom in the spaces below to answer this joke:

Who did Frankenstein's monster bring to the dance?

JOUST

LOFTY

NERVE

YODEL

KILNS

ALOHA

PRESS

SANDY

BRAID

ETHER

CRASH

OLIVE

IVORY

DIGIT

A	L	O	H	A

Write the highlighted letters here: **H** _ _ _ _ _ _ _ _ _ _

Sports!

Find and circle the 20 words listed below. The hidden words can read forward, backward, up, down, and diagonally in all directions.

```
S Q U A S H V H A W U D
I E L O Y B G U R C R V
N H U T L N R E C C O S
N F V V P O S E H R W U
E L T L K T P G E I U M
T O H G L N N G R C N O
A G N I V I D N Y K G I
R F N A F M C I Z E N B
A G I R C D V C L T I I
K J U D O A D N H H X H
P S L L A B Y E L L O V
G Y E O U D C F Y H B Y
```

GOLF
JUDO
POLO
SUMO

CANOE
RUGBY
BOXING
DIVING

KARATE
ROWING
SOCCER
SQUASH

TENNIS
ARCHERY
CRICKET
FENCING

SURFING
BADMINTON
WRESTLING
VOLLEYBALL

Out of School

Fill in the boxes in the BLANK GRID by copying exactly what you see in the same-numbered boxes in the SCRAMBLED GRID.

SCRAMBLED GRID

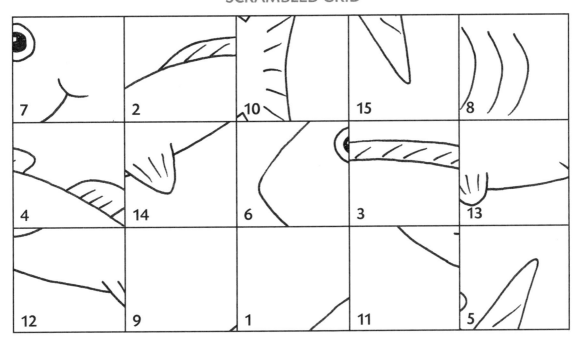

BLANK GRID

1	2	3	4	5
6	7	8	9	10
11	12	13	14	15

Moon Munchies

Put the 11 words into the grid in alphabetical order. We did the
first one to get you started. Then write the highlighted letters
from top to bottom in the spaces below to answer this joke:

How do you know when the moon has had enough to eat?

STALK

DEMON

HITCH

ENTER

CHIMP

AWAKE

QUAFF

ROGUE

JESTS

VAULT

GRIND

A	W	A	K	E

munch
munch

Write the highlighted letters here:

W _ _ _ _ _ ' _

_ _ _ _

HOME score:

HOOP

VISITOR score:

Penny Hoops

Here's a fun game of basketball
you can play with a penny!

1 POINT

1 POINT

1. Place a penny on one of the brown circles or anywhere in the yellow 3-POINT ZONE

2. Put a finger on the penny, close your eyes, then slide it toward to the hoop.

3. Stop sliding whenever you want, remove your finger, then open your eyes.

4. A penny completely in the hoop (not touching the red line) scores the number of points on your starting spot. Play to 21, alone or with a friend.

2 POINTS

2 POINTS

2 POINTS

3-POINT ZONE

Moon Meeting

There are 10 differences between the moonscape on this page and the one on the next page. Can you find and circle all 10 of them?

What's the Dif'?

The answer to this joke is written using a simple code.

First, circle each letter that's immediately to the right of a B. We did the first one to get you started. Then write the circled letters (starting at the top and reading left to right) in the spaces below to answer this joke:

What's the difference between here and there?

O B (T) G V M O U J M F W

A M N B H U N Z U X Y U

T Q N M B E X O V C E W

I G C Z M H Q E S M E X

E M B L L J U K X S Z A

R U X D O B E R K Q O R

M F V R Q W B T R W K J

Z Q E N C O L P Z B T I

O S M B E X S R D Q R K

A B R S L Z M G E D O Y

X M E E Q E N R V I Z R

G X Z M B T Y Q M S K S

Write the circled letters here:

T _ _ _   _ _ _ _ _ _   _

Root for Trees

There are seven questions on the left, and seven joke answers on the right.
Match them up by writing the correct number in each space.

What kind of tree can fit in your hand?

A. ___

What did the trees wear to the beach?

B. ___

What did the beaver say to the tree?

C. ___

What did the little tree say to the big bully tree?

D. ___

What kind of tree has the most friends?

E. ___

What is the tastiest kind of tree?

F. ___

How do you identify a dogwood tree?

G. ___

1. Nice gnawing you.

2. By its bark.

3. A palm tree.

4. A pastry.

5. Poplar.

6. Leaf me alone.

7. Swimming trunks.

Start Walking

Use the clues to write one letter in each square. We did the first one to get you started. We also included the alphabet at the bottom to help with some of the clues. When you're done, read across to find the answer to this joke:

Where do you send a shoe in the summer?

The first word:

1. The letter before C
2. The letter that looks like a zero
3. The letter repeated in BOOK
4. The letter that is halfway between O and Y

The second word:

5. The middle letter of PRINCIPAL
6. The letter that's the best grade on a homework assignment
7. The letter that looks like an upside-down W
8. The letter that's repeated in PUMPING

1 B	2	3	4
5	6	7	8

ABCDEFGHIJKLMNOPQRSTUVWXYZ

School Time

There are seven questions on the left, and seven joke answers on the right.
Match them up by writing the correct number in each space.

What's the worst thing about a school cafeteria?

A. ___

How do you get straight A's?

B. ___

What do elves learn in school?

C. ___

When do you eat at astronaut school?

D. ___

Why were the teacher's eyes crossed?

E. ___

What do you do if a teacher rolls her eyes at you?

F. ___

Why did the teacher write instructions on the window?

G. ___

This End Up

Astronaut School

1. The elf-abet.

2. Pick them up and roll them back.

3. So they would be clear.

4. The food.

5. At launch time.

6. Draw them with a ruler.

7. She couldn't control her pupils.

Pool Cat

Put the 10 words into the grid in alphabetical order. We did the first one to get you started. Then write the highlighted letters from top to bottom in the spaces below to answer this joke:

What kind of cat likes the water?

GECKO

NIPPY

LATCH

CRANE

BREAK

TASTY

FLOOR

PLUSH

RESET

MOODY

B	R	E	A	K

Write the highlighted letters here:

A __

__ __ __ __ __ - __ __ __ __

Rib-Tickler

A rib-tickler is a funny joke. One that's so funny it gets inside you and tickles your ribs. It might require a sidesplitting joke to get in there.

Your job is to write down as many words as possible using just the letters in RIB-TICKLER. No proper nouns and at least THREE letters long. OK, go!

9 WORDS — IT'S FUNNY HOW GOOD YOU ARE!

_____   _____   _____

_____   _____   _____

_____   _____   _____

18 WORDS — IT'S EVEN FUNNIER HOW GOOD YOU ARE!!

_____   _____   _____

_____   _____   _____

_____   _____   _____

20 OR MORE — IT'S EVEN FUNNIER HOW GREAT YOU ARE!!!

_____   _____   _____

_____   _____   _____

Whazzit?

The answer to this joke is written using a simple code.

First, circle each letter that's immediately to the right of an L. We did the first one to get you started. Then write the circled letters (starting at the top and reading left to right) in the spaces below to answer this joke:

What has four wheels and flies?

A Q W A R O Z Q E L A B
L G F D M I B V M N I X
K R D Q V A V P L A O Z
F E L R O Y X F N V M E
N R P I T L B D F T V E
N R L A W P H R W L G F
H S E N L E O U J F E W
V L T T Q U N Z U X Y U
B Q N V S U D L R C F D
I G C Z E H Q E F E L U
E L C Q T J F A X B P Z
R G L K M R U Y Q M V F

Write the circled letters here:

A _ _ _ _ _ _ _ _   _ _ _ _ _

98

Money Bags

Here's a fun game for 2-4 players. Players take turns. On each turn, draw one short line that connects two dots. When a rectangle is completed, surrounding a bag of money, mark your initials on it. The player who collects the most money bags wins!

Running Home

Put the 10 words into the grid in alphabetical order. We did the first one to get you started. Then write the highlighted letters from top to bottom in the spaces below to answer this joke:

Which baseball players leave almost as soon as they arrive?

UPSET

HURRY

FRONT

INTRO

TEPEE

JESTS

ETHER

MATCH

AISLE

OZONE

A	I	S	L	E

Hey, I gotta go.

Write the highlighted letters here: **S** _ _ _ _ _ _ _ _ _ _

Snow People

Which one of these drawings is exactly the same as the ORIGINAL?
Look carefully and circle the one that is exactly the same.

ORIGINAL

1

2

3

4

5

Too Cool for School

Find and circle the 20 words listed below. The hidden words can read forward, backward, up, down, and diagonally in all directions.

```
F E F R E H C A E T A V
Y D K P H W I C M P N W
D A E R E I N S K R N X
U R U I O E B K T O T Y
T G C N I W J M S O L W
S C I C G P E S Q M R S
W Q S I O V E M A Q H Y
M P U P I L S K O O B D
E W M A T H L S V H D Z
B M Y L R B G E A H W P
I W G A H T T D G L L A
R X J H S I L G N E C X
```

ART	MATH	GRADE	LESSON	SCIENCE
GYM	READ	MUSIC	COLLEGE	TEACHER
BOOK	ROOM	PUPIL	ENGLISH	HOMEWORK
DESK	CLASS	STUDY	HISTORY	PRINCIPAL

Smellfungus

A smellfungus is a person who finds fault with everything —
you know, like someone who thinks everything smells like fungus!

Your job is to write down as many words as possible using just the letters in
SMELLFUNGUS No proper nouns and at least THREE letters long. OK, go!

9 WORDS — NOT VERY GOOD!

_____ _____ _____

_____ _____ _____

_____ _____ _____

18 WORDS — NOT GOOD AT ALL!!

_____ _____ _____

_____ _____ _____

_____ _____ _____

20 OR MORE — OH, THIS IS EVEN WORSE!!!

_____ _____ _____

_____ _____ _____

So Long, Soccer

There are seven questions on the left, and seven joke answers on the right.
Match them up by writing the correct number in each space.

Where's the best place to buy a soccer uniform?

A. ____

What's a ghost's favorite soccer position?

B. ____

Why is Cinderella a lousy soccer player?

C. ____

What do grasshoppers like to watch more than soccer?

D. ____

How do soccer players stay cool during games?

E. ____

What runs around a soccer field but never moves?

F. ____

Why was the soccer field wet after the game?

G. ____

1. They stand near the fans.

2. New Jersey.

3. A fence.

4. Ghoul keeper.

5. She always runs away from the ball.

6. The players dribbled all over it.

7. Cricket.

What's the Connection?

Use the clues to write one letter in each square. We did the first one to get you started. We also included the alphabet at the bottom to help with some of the clues. When you're done, read across to find the answer to this joke:

What do Alexander the Great and Kermit the Frog have in common?

The first word:

1. The middle letter of ASK
2. The letter that comes 5 letters before F
3. The letter that's in TAME but not EAT
4. The letter that's repeated in SQUEEZE

The second word:

5. The letter that's both before and after an E in CEMENT
6. The repeated letter in INITIAL
7. The last letter of GROUND
8. The 4th letter of the alphabet
9. The letter in AIL that's not a vowel
10. The letter in STRENGTH that is a vowel

The third word:

11. The letter that comes 3 letters before Q
12. The letter that's in ANGRIEST but not STINGER
13. The letter between L and N
14. The middle letter in DANDELION

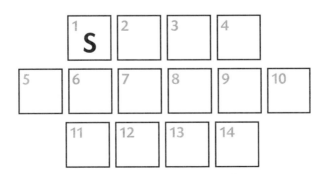

ABCDEFGHIJKLMNOPQRSTUVWXYZ

You Can Lick 'Em

Use the word and picture clues to fill in the answers, one letter per square.

If you don't know an answer, try filling in ones nearby or that go in the opposite direction.

1-Down

ACROSS

1 Green, clinging plant that can grow on buildings
4 How the third letter of the alphabet could be spelled out
5 People who write things like "Violets are blue, I love you"
7 Curved path a softball follows after being hit
8 Body part that feels pain (such as in a tooth)
11 One that sticks out on either side of the head
12 Denim pants
14 Limb that's inside a sleeve
15 Crazy or goofy
18 Part used to row a canoe
19 Camping structures used for sleeping
21 Cheer at a bullfight
22 Gives an approval

DOWN

1 They're made of a scoop or many piled on top of each other
2 Dog or cat doctor, for short
3 The opposite of "no"
5 An egg is fried in it on a stove
6 Gold, silver, or iron is a type of this valuable rock
9 Big moving truck
10 Hospital areas where people go for emergency treatment (for short)
12 Bony part of your head that contains your chin and teeth
13 Important time period
16 Kit-___ candy bar
17 365-day periods (abbreviation)
19 Also
20 Antlered animal that's in between a deer and a moose in size

19-Across

9-Down
Movers

R-I-G-H-T

The right way to solve this maze is to spell RIGHT!
It may look easy, but there's only one way to do it.

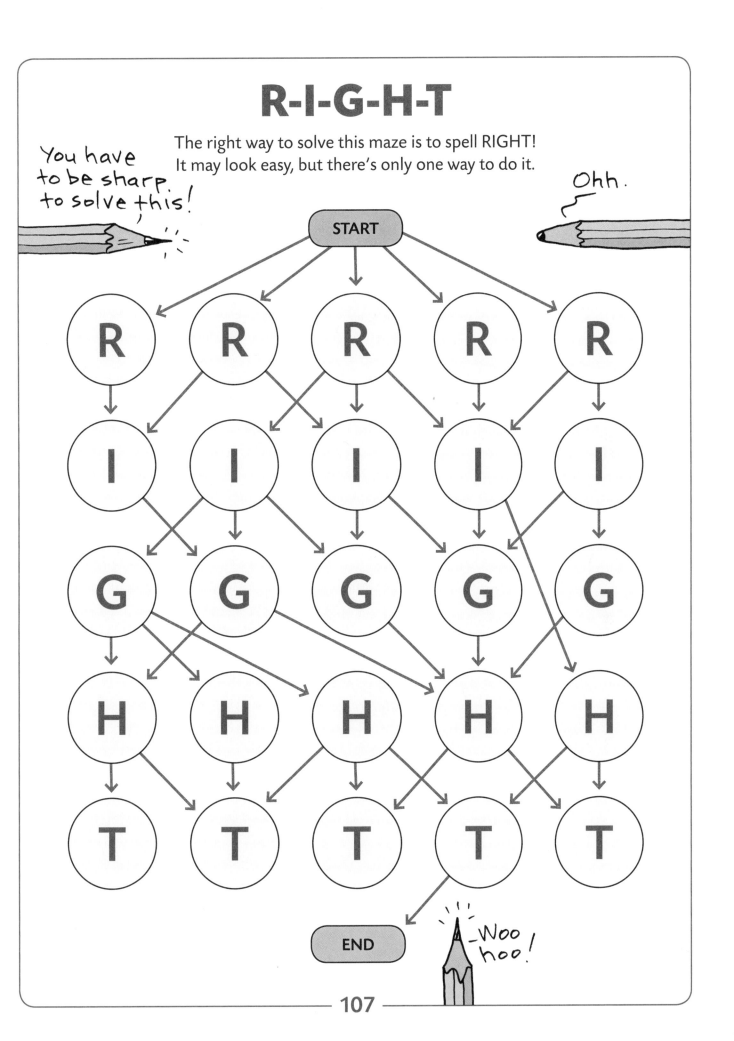

Wild and Woolly

The answer to this joke is written using a simple code.

First, circle each letter that's immediately to the right of an S. We did the first one to get you started. Then write the circled letters (starting at the top and reading left to right) in the spaces below to answer this joke:

Where do sheep watch their videos?

A Q W A R O Z Q E N V B
S Ⓞ F D M I B V M N I X
K R D Q V A V L S N L Z
F E E D O Y X F N V L E
N R P I T S E D F T V E
N R Q S W P H R W K J F
H S E N G E O U J F E W
V N S T Q U N Z U X Y U
B Q N V S U D O B C F D
I G C Z E H Q E F E S B
E S E Q L J F A X B P Z
R G X Z M R U Y Q M V F

Write the circled letters here:

O _   _ _ _ _ _ _ _

Swim Team

Which one of these drawings is exactly the same as the ORIGINAL?
Look carefully and circle the one that is exactly the same.

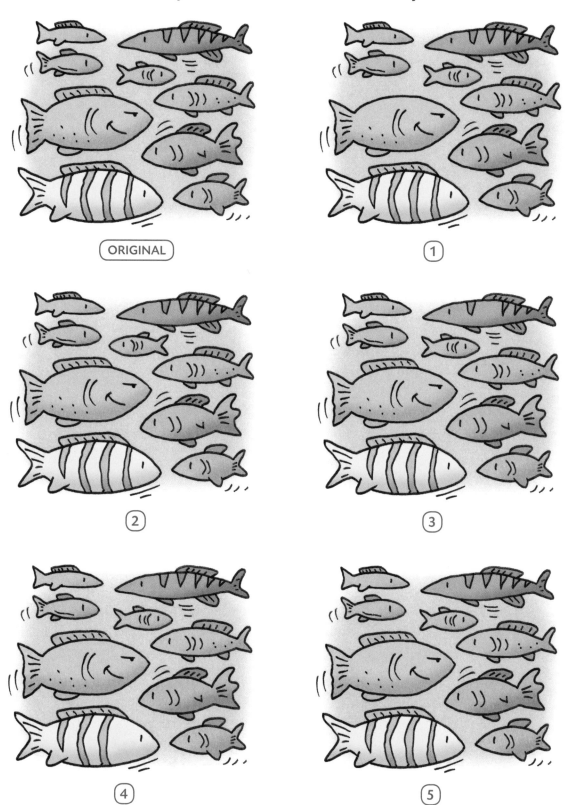

ORIGINAL

1

2

3

4

5

Teacher

What more noble job is there — spending day after day making
kids smarter and more interested in the world. Right?

Your job is to write down as many words as possible using just the letters in
TEACHER. No proper nouns and at least THREE letters long. OK, go!

9 WORDS – YOU GET A GOLD STAR!

_____ _____ _____

_____ _____ _____

_____ _____ _____

18 WORDS – YOU GET TWO GOLD STARS!!

_____ _____ _____

_____ _____ _____

_____ _____ _____

20 OR MORE – YOU'RE STUDENT OF THE WEEK!!!

_____ _____ _____

_____ _____ _____

U.S. States

Find and circle the 15 states listed below. The hidden words can read forward, backward, up, down, and diagonally in all directions.

```
K Y H A T U Y Y J M S R
Y Y E T D Y X N I T A O S
N N D I E P M V S C B Z
A E V R I L R N M N C V
G B K O E N A N D I W G
I R W L J K D W I F F O
H A Y F F U Y I A Z O J
C S O C C K I T A R A A
I K M O A D A V E N E O
M A I N E K Q G C X A Q
U H N N G E O R G I A Q
O J G S G N O P I E J S
```

IOWA	MAINE	NEVADA	GEORGIA	DELAWARE
OHIO	TEXAS	OREGON	INDIANA	MICHIGAN
UTAH	KANSAS	FLORIDA	WYOMING	NEBRASKA

Summer Fun

There are seven questions on the left, and seven joke answers on the right.
Match them up by writing the correct number in each space.

Where do sharks go on vacation?

A. ____

Why don't mummies go on vacations?

B. ____

Why don't elephants buy suitcases for traveling?

C. ____

What does the Sun drink out of?

D. ____

What's the best day to get a sunburn at the beach?

E. ____

Where does a canoe go when it's not feeling well?

F. ____

Why did the miniature golfers bring extra socks?

G. ____

1. Fry day.

2. They're afraid they'll relax and unwind.

3. To the dock.

4. Finland.

5. They already have trunks.

6. In case they get a hole in one.

7. Sun glasses.

A Short Month

Put the 13 words into the grid in alphabetical order. We did the first one to get you started. Then write the highlighted letters from top to bottom in the spaces below to answer this joke:

Why did the guy get fired at the calendar factory?

FLOCK

BEGIN

ROBOT

WHIFF

DROVE

HIKED

CATER

JUDGE

PAYER

AHEAD

THEFT

IDEAL

MEALS

Write the highlighted letters here:

H _ _ _ _ _ _

_ _ _ _ _ _

A	H	E	A	D

Tell a Phony

The answer to this joke is written using a simple code.

First, circle each letter that's immediately to the right of a P. We did the first one to get you started. Then write the circled letters (starting at the top and reading left to right) in the spaces below to answer this joke:

How do you figure out how old a smartphone is?

Write the circled letters here:

C O U N T   I T S   R I N G S

Squirt Ahead

Find the one messy mustard path that runs from Start to End.
Go ahead. Show us you're a hot dog!

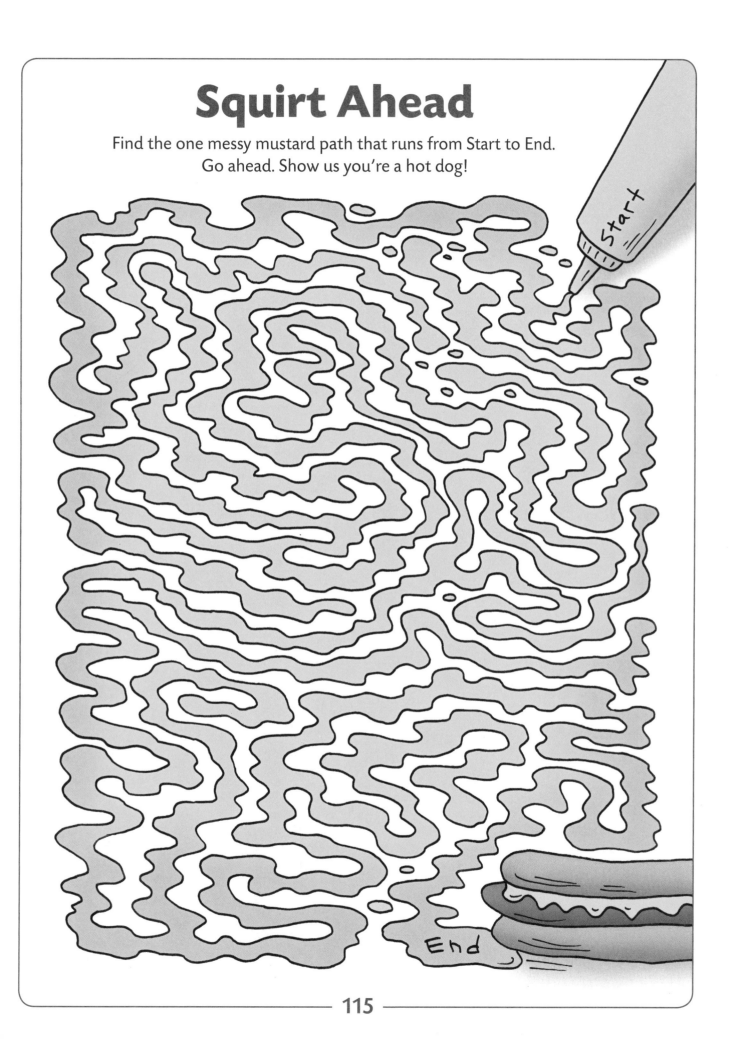

Various Vehicles

There are seven questions on the left, and seven joke answers on the right.
Match them up by writing the correct number in each space.

Who DIDN'T invent the airplane?

A. ____

What did the tornado say to the car?

B. ____

What would you call a country where everyone drives red cars?

C. ____

What do you get if you group many houseboats together?

D. ____

What sound does a bulldozer make?

E. ____

How do trains hear each other?

F. ____

What has one horn and gives milk?

G. ____

1. Want to go for a spin?

2. A township.

3. A milk truck.

4. With their engine-ears.

5. The wrong brothers.

6. The same as a cow that's dozing.

7. A red car-nation.

'Snow Joke

Put the 10 words into the grid in alphabetical order. We did the first one to get you started. Then write the highlighted letters from top to bottom in the spaces below to answer this joke:

What do you call a snowman in Florida?

KINGS

LAPEL

MOURN

FLUBS

BEACH

VALUE

YIELD

HABIT

PEDAL

RIDGE

Write the highlighted letters here:

A _ _ _ _

_ _ _ _ _ _

B	E	A	C	H

Hammer Time

The answer to this joke is written using a simple code.

First, circle each letter that's immediately to the right of an H. We did the first one to get you started. Then write the circled letters (starting at the top and reading left to right) in the spaces below to answer this joke:

What nail should you never hit with a hammer?

M F V R Q H (Y) O R W K J

H O E N B O L P Z B M I

K Y Z G V M H U J B F W

A H R I H F N Z U X Y U

B Q N M T U X H I C E W

I G C H N I Q E S M E X

E M I Q L H G K X S Z A

A H E S L Z M G E D O Y

X M E E Q E N R V H R R

H N Z M R U Y Q M S K S

C U H A O U M R K Q O B

T S M H I X S R D Q H L

Write the circled letters here:

_Y_ _ _ _   _ _ _ _ _ _ _ _ _ _

Say Cheese!

Which one of these drawings is exactly the same as the ORIGINAL?
Look carefully and circle the one that is exactly the same.

ORIGINAL

①

②

③

④

⑤

Solutions

Coming Right Up

The answer to this joke is written using a simple code.

First, circle each letter that's immediately to the right of a V. We did the first one to get you started. Then write the circled letters (starting at the top and reading left to right) in the spaces below to answer this joke:

What do you serve but never eat?

```
B U X D O U M V (T) Q O B
V (E) N R Q W I O R W K J
O V (N) E M O U J B F W
V (N) I Q U N Z U X Y U
B Q N V (I) U X O B C E W
I G C Z M H Q E V (S) E T
E M I Q L J U K X S Z A
Z Q E N V (B) L P Z B M I
B S M N I X S R D Q V (A)
V (L) Q S L Z M G E D O Y
X M E V (L) E N R P I Z R
G B Z M R U Y Q M V (S) S
```

Write the circled letters here:

T E N N I S   B A L L S

1

Bats in the Belfry

Which one of these drawings is exactly the same as the ORIGINAL? Look carefully and circle the one that is exactly the same.

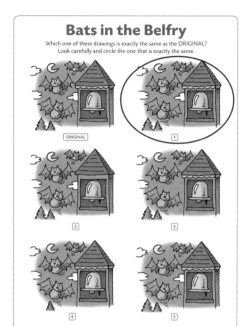

2

Amoeboid

An amoeba is a really tiny, blobby-shaped creature. Only people with microscopes can see them. And amoeboid (UH-MEE-BOID) means "resembling an amoeba."

Your job is to write down as many words as possible using just the letters in AMOEBOID. No proper nouns and at least THREE letters long. OK, go!

HERE'S OUR LIST OF COMMON WORDS
If you think of others that are in the dictionary, count them!

ADO	DIM	BODE	OBOE
AID	DOE	BOOM	ABIDE
AIM	MAD	DAME	ABODE
BAD	MOB	DIME	ADOBE
BED	MOO	DOME	AIMED
BID	ODE	DOOM	BOOED
BOA	AIDE	IDEA	MEDIA
BOO	AMID	MADE	MOOED
DAB	BEAD	MAID	BOOMED
DAM	BEAM	MODE	
DIE	BIDE	MOOD	

3

Captain Overboard!

Use the clues to write one letter in each square. We did the first one to get you started. We also included the alphabet at the bottom to help with some of the clues. When you're done, read across to find the answer to this joke:

What does the pirate Bluebeard become when he falls in the Red Sea?

1. The letter before N
2. The 4th letter in BREAD
3. The letter that looks like a P, but with one additional line
4. The letter that looks the most like an egg
5. The letter that's in CLOAK but not LACK
6. The letter that looks like a Z turned on its side
7. The letter that's halfway between A and I
8. The middle letter in SCREWDRIVER

M A R O O N E D

ABCDEFGHIJKLMNOPQRSTUVWXYZ

4

American History

There are seven questions on the left, and seven joke answers on the right. Match them up by writing the correct number in each space.

Where was the Declaration of Independence signed?   A. **3**

How were the first Americans like ants?   B. **5**

Where did the pilgrims land when they came to America?   C. **1**

Why does the Statue of Liberty stand in New York Harbor?   D. **7**

What was worn at the Boston Tea Party?   E. **6**

What did the cherry tree say after George Washington chopped it down?   F. **2**

What was the most popular dance in 1776?   G. **4**

1. On their feet.
2. I'm stumped.
3. At the bottom.
4. The Indepen-dance.
5. They lived in colonies.
6. T-shirts.
7. Because it can't sit down.

5

Bowing Bug

Put the 14 words into the grid in alphabetical order. We did the first one to get you started. Then write the highlighted letters from top to bottom in the spaces below to answer this joke:

What bug always gives thanks before eating?

FINAL

NEIGH

TITLE

JOEYS

DIARY

ALARM

PUMPS

MOUNT

WASTE

QUAIL

LIMIT

RINSE

UNITE

CHAPS

A	L	A	R	M
C	H	A	P	S
D	I	A	R	Y
F	I	N	A	L
J	O	E	Y	S
L	I	M	I	T
M	O	U	N	T
N	E	I	G	H
P	U	M	P	S
Q	U	A	I	L
R	I	N	S	E
T	I	T	L	E
U	N	I	T	E
W	A	S	T	E

Write the highlighted letters here:

A   P R A Y I N G
M A N T I S

6

At the Fair

Find and circle the 20 words listed below. The hidden words can read forward, backward, up, down, and diagonally in all directions.

```
S Y L M G B P N M W F J
A U L O J U T E K E P T
J I D L O M I H D T I B
X X V L V P J I E C H G
W O L I N E R N K M G O
D H L R A R O E K G E D
U K A H N C T D T E N T
E I D T O A V M R Z O R
N D O N B R S T A R E H
V D S X B Z Z R I J R L
O I X C I U L H N J A S
C E Z I R P W H E E L Y
```

JAM	RIDE	THEME	HOT DOG	TICKET
PIE	SODA	TRAIN	KIDDIE	PRETZEL
LINE	TENT	WHEEL	RIBBON	SNO-CONE
LOOP	PRIZE	WHIRL	THRILL	BUMPER CAR

7

Dribbling Allowed

Use the word and picture clues to fill in the answers, one letter per square.

If you don't know an answer, try filling in ones nearby or that go in the opposite direction.

ACROSS
1 Body of water that's smaller than a sea but bigger than a lake
4 You ___ Here (phrase on a shopping mall map)
5 Hockey goalies wear them to protect their faces
7 Fluid in a pen
8 Had some food
9 Small child (it's a word that's spelled the same forward and backward)
12 Metal rod you grab to do chin-ups
13 Like a rowboat that's taking on water
15 Sick
16 Open from dawn '___ dusk

DOWN
1 It's dribbled on a court
2 Noah's boat in the Bible
3 The opposite of "no"
5 Girls name that's spelled with the letters in AIM
6 Little insect with tunnels in the ground and a hill for an entrance
10 Tree that makes acorns
11 Make an attempt
13 She ___ the candles on the cake (past tense of "light")
14 Cotton gin inventor Whitney or NFL quarterback Mannin

8

Bloviate

Bloviate (blow-vee-ate) means to speak a lot and to use a lot of big words. Funny thing is, one who bloviates often doesn't have much worth saying!

Your job is to write down as many words as possible using just the letters in BLOVIATE. No proper nouns and at least THREE letters long. OK, go!

HERE'S OUR LIST OF COMMON WORDS
If you think of others that are in the dictionary, count them!

AIL	OAT	BAIT	LOVE	ABOVE
ALE	OIL	BALE	OVAL	ALIVE
ATE	TAB	BATE	TAIL	BLEAT
BAT	TEA	BEAT	TALE	BLOAT
BET	TIE	BELT	TEAL	OLIVE
BIT	TIL	BILE	TILE	TABLE
BOA	TOE	BITE	TOIL	VALET
BOT	VAT	BLOT	VEAL	VIOLA
EAT	VET	BOAT	VEIL	VITAL
LAB	VIA	BOIL	VETO	VIABLE
LET	VIE	BOLT	VIAL	VIOLET
LIE	ABLE	EVIL	VIBE	VIOLATE
LIT	ALOE	LATE	VILE	
LOB	ALTO	LIVE	VOLT	
LOT	BAIL	LOBE	VOTE	

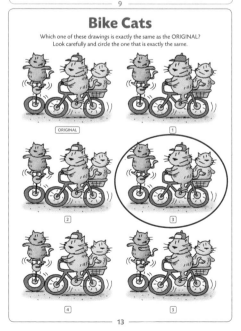

9

Out of Africa

Cross off every letter that appears MORE THAN TWICE in the grid. Then write the leftover letters (starting at the top and reading left to right) in the spaces below to find the answer to this question:

What is the capital of Botswana?

Write the leftover letters here:

C A P I T A L   B

12

Bike Cats

Which one of these drawings is exactly the same as the ORIGINAL? Look carefully and circle the one that is exactly the same.

13

Fun at the Fair

There are 10 differences between the county fair scene on this page and the one on the next page. Can you find and circle all 10 of them?

15

123

Cool Ghoul

The answer to this joke is written using a simple code.

First, circle each letter that's immediately to the right of an X. We did the first one to get you started. Then write the circled letters (starting at the top and reading left to right) in the spaces below to answer this joke:

What do you get if you cross a snowman and a vampire?

```
I  G  C  Z  M  X (F) E  S  M  E  V
E  M  I  Q  L  J  U  K  G  S  Z  A
B  U  R  X (R) U  M  R  K  Q  O  B
M  F  V  R  Q  W  I  O  R  W  K  J
Z  Q  E  N  B  O  L  X (O) B  M  I
B  S  M  N  I  P  X (S) D  Q  R  K
A  X (T) S  L  Z  M  G  E  D  O  Y
B  M  E  E  X (B) N  R  V  I  Z  R
G  F  Z  M  R  U  Y  Q  M  X (I) S
O  Y  Z  G  V  M  O  U  J  B  F  W
A  M  N  X (T) U  N  Z  U  M  Y  U
B  Q  N  M  T  U  X (E) V  C  E  W
```

Write the circled letters here:

F R O S T B I T E

Bufflehead

A bufflehead is a kind of diving duck with a big head.
A male bufflehead can puff out its head feathers to make it even bigger!

Your job is to write down as many words as possible using just the letters in BUFFLEHEAD No proper nouns and at least THREE letters long. OK, go!

HERE'S OUR LIST OF COMMON WORDS
If you think of others that are in the dictionary, count them!

ALE	HUB	DEAL	HALE	BLEED
BAD	HUE	DUAL	HALF	BLUFF
BED	LAB	DUEL	HAUL	ELUDE
BEE	LAD	DUFF	HEAD	FABLE
BUD	LED	FADE	HEAL	BAFFLE
DAB	LEE	FEED	HEED	BEHALF
DUB	ABLE	FEEL	HEEL	BEHEAD
DUE	BALD	FEUD	HELD	BEHELD
EEL	BALE	FLAB	HUED	DUFFEL
ELF	BEAD	FLEA	HUFF	FABLED
FAD	BEEF	FLED	LADE	FUELED
FED	BLED	FLEE	LAUD	HAULED
FEE	BLUE	FLUB	LEAD	HEALED
FLU	BUFF	FLUE	LEAF	BAFFLED
HAD	DEAF	FUEL	BLADE	HEEDFUL

Clean Ocean

Use the clues to write one letter in each square. We did the first one to get you started. We also included the alphabet at the bottom to help with some of the clues. When you're done, read across to find the answer to this joke:

**Who keeps the
ocean floor tidy?**

1. The letter that comes 2 letters before O
2. The letter that comes 6th in PRINCESS
3. The letter that's halfway between L and X
4. The letter that's repeated in MEMORY
5. The letter that's in both BALL and CHAIN
6. The letter that's a single straight line
7. The 4th letter of the alphabet
8. The letter that appears only once in TOOTS

M E R - M A I D S

A B C D E F G H I J K L M N O P Q R S T U V W X Y Z

Don't Blow It

Put the 10 words into the grid in alphabetical order. We did the first one to get you started. Then write the highlighted letters from top to bottom in the spaces below to answer this joke:

What kind of tests do balloons fear most?

PLAZA
TRASH   APPLE
LATIN   KAPUT
QUEEN   CLOCK
IRAQI   MAIZE
   GUPPY

```
A P P L E
C L O C K
G U P P Y
I R A Q I
K A P U T
L A T I N
M A I Z E
P L A Z A
Q U E E N
T R A S H
```

Write the highlighted letters here:

P O P
Q U I Z Z E S

A Phew Jokes

There are seven questions on the left, and seven joke answers on the right.
Match them up by writing the correct number in each space.

How do you stop a skunk from smelling?   A. 2

Why did the skunk bring toilet paper to the party?   B. 7

What did the judge say when a skunk came into the courtroom?   C. 1

Why are skunks smart?   D. 6

What do you get when you cross a bear and a skunk?   E. 3

What do all skunk jokes have in common?   F. 4

What do you call a flying skunk?   G. 5

1. Odor in the court.
2. Plug up its nose.
3. Winnie the P.U.
4. They stink.
5. A smell-icopter.
6. Because they have lots of scents.
7. Because it was a party pooper.

124

Birthday Time!

Find and circle the 20 words listed below. The hidden words can read forward, backward, up, down, and diagonally in all directions.

```
E L B A T J D G T J A I
Y T R A P J A C S O N T
D D A S N O O L L A B T
N V P T P N P J E O O E
A U O R Y I E W Z W W F
C W U E O K H R T I L N
A E T A L P A C E K A O
K X Q M D A T Z R R A C
E X A E E N S A P L U W
L D C R R P D R I N K S
L X U S R O V A F Z K C
L E K B S S E I K H A D
```

BOWL	SODA	OLDER	BANNER	BALLOONS
CAKE	CANDY	PARTY	DRINKS	CONFETTI
CUPS	CHIPS	PLATE	FAVORS	PRETZELS
HATS	CLOWN	TABLE	NAPKIN	STREAMERS

Furry Friend

Use the word and picture clues to
fill in the answers, one letter per square.

If you don't know an answer, try filling in ones
nearby or that go in the opposite direction.

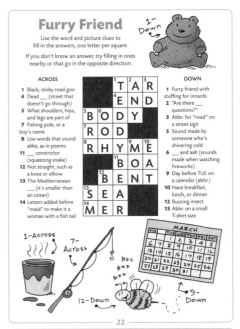

ACROSS

1 Black, sticky road goo
4 Dead ___ (street that doesn't go through)
5 What shoulders, hips, and legs are part of
7 Fishing pole, or a boy's name
8 Use words that sound alike, as in poems
11 ___ constrictor (squeezing snake)
12 Not straight, such as a knee or elbow
13 The Mediterranean ___ (it's smaller than an ocean)
14 Letters added before "maid" to make it a woman with a fish tail

DOWN

1 Furry friend with stuffing for innards
2 "Are there ___ questions?"
3 Abbr. for "road" on a street sign
5 Sound made by someone who's shivering cold
6 ___ and aah (sounds made when watching fireworks)
9 Day before TUE on a calendar (abbr.)
10 Have breakfast, lunch, or dinner
12 Buzzing insect
13 Abbr. on a small T-shirt size

Grid:
```
T A R
  E N D
B O D Y
R O D
R H Y M E
    B O A
  B E N T
S E A
M E R
```

1-Across
7-Across
12-Down
9-Down

22

Doodle Mania

Find a path through this
crazy maze from Start to End.

Start

End

23

Crudivore

This isn't pronounced like you may think. It's CROO-DA-VORE.
It means someone who eats only raw food.

Your job is to write down as many words as possible using just the letters in
CRUDIVORE. No proper nouns and at least THREE letters long. OK, go!

HERE'S OUR LIST OF COMMON WORDS
If you think of others that are in the dictionary, count them!

COD	ROD	DOVE	COVER	ROVER
CUD	RUE	ICED	CRIED	VIDEO
CUE	VIE	OVER	CRIER	VOICE
DIE	CODE	REDO	CRUDE	CRUDER
DOE	CORD	RICE	CURED	CURVED
DUE	CORE	RIDE	CURVE	DEVOUR
DUO	COVE	RODE	DECOR	DRIVER
ERR	CRUD	ROVE	DIVER	RECORD
ICE	CUED	RUDE	DRIER	VOICED
IRE	CURD	RUED	DRIVE	COURIER
ODE	CURE	VICE	DROVE	CURRIED
ORE	DICE	VIED	ORDER	DIVORCE
OUR	DIRE	VOID	RECUR	
RED	DIVE	CIDER	RIDER	
REV	DOER	CORED	RIVER	
RID	DOUR	CORER	ROVED	

24

Copy Cat!

The answer to this joke is written using a simple code.

First, circle each letter that's immediately to the right of a C.
We did the first one to get you started. Then write the
circled letters (starting at the top and reading left to right)
in the spaces below to answer this joke:

What is every cat in the world always doing at the same time?

```
I G W Z O H Q E S C (G) X
C (R) I Q L J U K X S Z A
B J C (O) O U M R K Q O B
X M E E Q C (W) R V I Z R
G X Z M R U Y C (I) S K S
O Y C (N) V M O U J B F M
A M N I C (G) N Z U X Y U
V Q N M T U X C (O) W E J
M F V C (L) W I O R T K J
Z Q E N C (D) L P Z B M I
B S M N C (E) S R D Q A J
A C (R) S L Z M G E D O Y
```

Write the circled letters here:
G R O W I N G   O L D E R

25

Fairy Smelly

Use the clues to write one letter in each square. We did the first one to get
you started. We also included the alphabet at the bottom to help with some
of the clues. When you're done, read across to find the answer to this joke:

What do you call a fairy who won't take a bath?

The first word:

1. The letter that comes after R
2. The letter in TOSS-UP that's made with only straight lines
3. The letter that sounds like a body part you see with
4. The middle letter in THUNDER
5. The letter repeated in KENTUCKY
6. The letter missing in ABCDF
7. The letter that comes 5 letters after M

The second word:

8. The letter that's in both BIRD and BEE
9. The middle letter in SHELL
10. The letter between K and M
11. The letter halfway between H and P

S T I N K E R
B E L L

No thanks!

ABCDEFGHIJKLMNOPQRSTUVWXYZ

26

125

Gobbling

Put the 11 words into the grid in alphabetical order. We did the
first one to get you started. Then write the highlighted letters
from top to bottom in the spaces below to answer this joke:

*What are turkeys
thankful for on
Thanksgiving?*

CHESS
ZESTY
ANVIL
EAGLE
QUIET
KITES

NORTH
FRESH
MEANT
TRADE
WINCE

A	N	V	I	L	
C	H	E	S	S	
E	A	G	L	E	
F	R	E	S	H	
K	I	T	E	S	
M	E	A	N	T	
N	O	R	T	H	
Q	U	I	E	T	
T	R	A	D	E	
W	I	N	C	E	
Z	E	S	T	Y	

Thank you!

Write the highlighted letters here: **V E G E T A R I A N S**

27

Boat-igator

Which one of these drawings is exactly the same as the ORIGINAL?
Look carefully and circle the one that is exactly the same.

ORIGINAL

1

2

3

4

5

— 28 —

Critters

Find and circle the 20 words listed below. The hidden words can read forward, backward, up, down, and diagonally in all directions.

```
M O O S E B Q H E D R N
Q O S U I Q E K R U H M
D R N T I B B A R A U A
I R A K B Q Z C R K C R
E M K W E I K L D M J M
L S E F L Y R X U B M Y
A K R L E C E D H X G I
H U J O P I G C P T O C
W N B W H N O O C C A R
Q K O C A T D E E R T P
I F T I N S E C T D X S
K R E J T U R T L E L J
```

CAT	BIRD	HORSE	WHALE	RABBIT
DOG	DEER	MOOSE	INSECT	TURTLE
PIG	GOAT	SKUNK	LIZARD	RACCOON
BEAR	WOLF	SNAKE	MONKEY	ELEPHANT

— 29 —

Birthdays!

There are seven questions on the left, and seven joke answers on the right.
Match them up by writing the correct number in each space.

What do Columbus and Lincoln have in common?   A. 6

What goes up but never comes down?   B. 4

What do they serve at birthday parties in heaven?   C. 7

What do cats like to eat on their birthdays?   D. 5

What do you call a birthday present the day after you get it?   E. 1

Why are birthdays good for your health?   F. 2

Why do we put candles on top of a birthday cake?   G. 3

1. A birthday past.
2. The more you have, the longer you live.
3. It's hard to put them on the bottom.
4. Your age.
5. Cake and mice cream.
6. They were both born on holidays.
7. Angel food cake.

— 30 —

Going in Reverse

Use the word and picture clues to fill in the answers, one letter per square.

If you don't know an answer, try filling in ones nearby or that go in the opposite direction.

ACROSS
1 Not against (such as supporters of the home team)
4 What a basketball net is attached to
7 10 - 8 = ___
8 Girl's name (it's spelled the same forward and backward)
9 Piles of pancakes
11 Drink that's a lot like beer
12 "I didn't ___ (see) anything odd"
15 Two words said when getting married
16 Amaze
18 Word that means "for each," as in: Only one soda ___ person
19 Strawberry or tomato color

DOWN
1 Abbreviation for foot or fort
2 "Ouch, that hurts!" sounds
3 Spinning thing (it's spelled the same forward and backward)
4 Fast vehicle (it's spelled the same forward and backward; 2 words)
5 Black stuff squirted by an octopus
6 Mothers, for short
10 Aladdin hero
12 Small bite made by a puppy
13 Type of poem
14 Female sheep (it's spelled the same forward and backward)
17 Nickname for Edward

```
F O R | R I M
T W O | A N A
    S T A C K S
      A L E
N O T I C E
I D O | A W E
P E R | R E D
```

9-Across

19-Across

4-Down

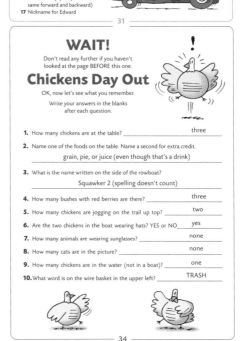

— 31 —

Don't Move!

Cross off every letter that appears MORE THAN TWICE in the grid.
Then write the leftover letters (starting at the top and reading left to right) in the spaces below to find the answer to this question:

What goes up and down and yet always stays in the same place?

S ... T ... A ... I ... R ... S

Write the leftover letters here:
S T A I R S

— 32 —

126

WAIT!

Don't read any further if you haven't looked at the page BEFORE this one.

Chickens Day Out

OK, now let's see what you remember.

Write your answers in the blanks after each question.

1. How many chickens are at the table? _____ three

2. Name one of the foods on the table. Name a second for extra credit.
_____ grain, pie, or juice (even though that's a drink)

3. What is the name written on the side of the rowboat?
_____ Squawker 2 (spelling doesn't count)

4. How many bushes with red berries are there? _____ three

5. How many chickens are jogging on the trail up top? _____ two

6. Are the two chickens in the boat wearing hats? YES or NO _____ yes

7. How many animals are wearing sunglasses? _____ none

8. How many cats are in the picture? _____ none

9. How many chickens are in the water (not in a boat)? _____ one

10. What word is on the wire basket in the upper left? _____ TRASH

— 34 —

Dots the Way

There are many ways to get from Start to End. But only one route visits just SEVEN red dots. The other routes visit more. Can you find it?

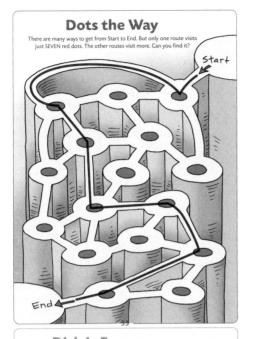

Start

End

35

Clowning Around

Which one of these drawings is exactly the same as the ORIGINAL?
Look carefully and circle the one that is exactly the same.

ORIGINAL

1

2

3

4

5

36

Dish Is Funny

The answer to this joke is written using a simple code.

First, circle each letter that's immediately to the right of a P. We did the first one to get you started. Then write the circled letters (starting at the top and reading left to right) in the spaces below to answer this joke:

What did the one plate say to the other?

P Ⓓ E F Q E N R V I Z R
G X Ⓘ R U Y Q M S K S
R Y Z G V P Ⓝ U J B F W
L M N I Q U N Z U X P Ⓝ
P Ⓔ N M T U X O V C E W
I G C P Ⓡ H Q E S M E X
Z Q E N B O P Ⓘ Z B M I
T S M N P Ⓢ S R I Q R K
A U Q P Ⓞ Z M G E F O Y
E M I Q L J P Ⓝ X S Z A
G U X M O U M R K P Ⓜ B
M F V P Ⓔ W I O R W K J

Write the circled letters here:

<u>D I N N E R</u>   <u>I S</u>   <u>O N</u>   <u>M E</u>

38

Folderol

Folderol (FALL-DE-RALL) is nonsense or a lot of silly fuss made about something that's total nonsense.

Your job is to write down as many words as possible using just the letters in FOLDEROL. No proper nouns and at least THREE letters long. OK, go!

HERE'S OUR LIST OF COMMON WORDS
If you think of others that are in the dictionary, count them!

ELF	ROD	FOOL	DROLL
FED	ROE	FORD	DROOL
FOE	DELL	FORE	FLOOD
FOR	DOER	LORD	FLOOR
FRO	DOLE	LORE	OLDER
LED	DOLL	ODOR	RODEO
ODE	DOOR	REDO	FOLDER
OLD	FELL	RODE	FOOLED
ORE	FLED	ROLE	ROLLED
RED	FOLD	ROLL	ROOFED
REF	FOOD	ROOF	FLOORED

39

Filling His Sack

Use the clues to write one letter in each square. We did the first one to get you started. We also included the alphabet at the bottom to help with some of the clues. When you're done, read across to find the answer to this joke:

Where does Santa go to buy potatoes?

1. The letter before J
2. The letter that's just a little better grade than an F
3. The 2nd, 4th, and 6th letter in PAJAMAS
4. The middle letter of MACHINE
5. The vowel that comes 4th in the alphabet
6. The letter that's in REACH but not RACE
7. The letter between N and P
8. The 7th letter of STRETCHED
9. The letter that comes 12 letters after C

I D A H O - H O - H O

ABCDEFGHIJKLMNOPQRSTUVWXYZ

40

I'm Not Moving!

Put the 12 words into the grid in alphabetical order. We did the first one to get you started. Then write the highlighted letters from top to bottom in the spaces below to answer this joke:

What has two legs but can't walk?

YEAST
MUMPS
AMAZE
BUMPS
HOOEY
TEETH
FRAIL
GUARD
DREAM
LIFTS
NAVAL
OWING

A	M	A	Z	E
B	U	M	P	S
D	R	E	A	M
F	R	A	I	L
G	U	A	R	D
H	O	O	E	Y
L	I	F	T	S
M	U	M	P	S
N	A	V	A	L
O	W	I	N	G
T	E	E	T	H
Y	E	A	S	T

Write the highlighted letters here:

<u>A   P A I R</u>
<u>O F   P A N T S</u>

41

127

Gimme Some Space

There are seven questions on the left, and seven joke answers on the right.
Match them up by writing the correct number in each space.

What is an astronaut's favorite part of a computer keyboard? A. 5

What did the alien cat say when it landed on Earth? B. 4

Where did the cow go after jumping over the moon? C. 6

Why is Saturn rich? D. 2

How do you know when the moon is going broke? E. 7

If an athlete gets athlete's foot what does an astronaut get? F. 1

How do you get a baby to sleep in space? G. 3

1. Mistletoe (missile toe).

2. Because it has lots of rings.

3. Rocket (rock it) to sleep.

4. Take me to your litter.

5. The space bar.

6. The Milky Way.

7. When it's down to its last quarter.

42

Flower Power

Find and circle the 20 words listed below. The hidden words can read forward, backward, up, down, and diagonally in all directions.

G	A	R	D	E	N	I	A	V	D	D	T
Y	Z	C	A	R	N	A	T	I	O	N	L
N	A	W	F	C	M	T	H	O	R	N	V
O	L	C	F	O	A	C	Q	T	U	I	V
E	E	S	O	R	R	T	U	S	V	P	S
P	A	L	D	O	I	C	U	L	C	C	V
A	B	A	I	O	G	C	D	L	M	G	Z
N	R	T	L	T	O	N	A	T	I	O	D
S	T	E	M	R	L	N	H	L	Z	P	M
Y	D	P	C	M	D	B	L	D	I	H	W
S	E	V	B	O	D	A	I	S	Y	L	Q
L	I	X	S	W	H	G	A	S	G	I	K

IRIS	BLOOM	PEONY	AZALEA	DAFFODIL
ROOT	DAISY	PETAL	CROCUS	GARDENIA
ROSE	LILAC	THORN	DAHLIA	MARIGOLD
STEM	PANSY	TULIP	ORCHID	CARNATION

43

Happy Times

Use the word and picture clues to fill in the answers, one letter per square.

If you don't know an answer, try filling in ones nearby or that go in the opposite direction.

ACROSS
1 The opposite of "good"
4 Cold cubes in the freezer
5 Witch's ___ (boiling mixture in a big pot)
6 Small house with bamboo walls and a palm tree roof
7 Gray leftover stuff in a fireplace
10 Little circle on top of an i or a j
11 Beautiful, white long-necked water bird
13 Give money when buying something
14 They're gained during a football game (abbr.)

DOWN
1 Once-a-year occasions with presents and cake
2 The highest card in a deck of cards
3 Little drops of water covering the grass early in the morning
5 Yellow vehicle for getting many kids to and from school
6 Laughed-out-loud word
8 Very long period of time
9 Abbr. following Main or Elm on a street sign
11 Secret agent
12 Gob of gum

Crossword answers: 1 BAD, 4 ICE, 5 BREW, 6 HUT, 7 ASHES, 10 DOT, 11 SWAN, 13 PAY, 14 YDS

44

Hop To It

Following the arrows, find the one path that visits each and every lily pad exactly once.

start

End!

45

Gasconade

Gasconade (GAS-CON-ADE) isn't some kind of fruity drink. It's just another word for boasting, such as: "His speech was filled with gasconade." Know anyone like that?

Your job is to write down as many words as possible using just the letters in GASCONADE. No proper nouns and at least THREE letters long. OK, go!

HERE'S OUR LIST OF COMMON WORDS
If you think of others that are in the dictionary, count them!

ACE	NAG	CASE	NODS	CASED
ADO	NOD	CODE	NOGS	CODES
ADS	NOG	COGS	NOSE	CONES
AGE	ODE	CONE	ODES	DANCE
AGO	ONE	CONS	ONCE	DEANS
AND	SAC	DEAN	ONES	NOSED
CAD	SAD	DENS	SAGA	OCEAN
CAN	SAG	DOES	SAGE	SCONE
COD	SEA	DOGS	SAND	SEDAN
COG	SEC	DONE	SANE	ADAGES
CON	SOD	DONS	SANG	AGENDA
DEN	SON	DOSE	SCAN	ASCEND
DOE	ACED	EGOS	SEND	CANOES
DOG	ACES	ENDS	SNAG	DANCES
DON	ACNE	EONS	SODA	DEACON
EGO	AGED	GOAD	SONG	DOSAGE
END	AGES	GODS	ADAGE	OCEANS
EON	CAGE	GOES	CAGED	SECOND
GAS	CANE	GONE	CAGES	AGENDAS
GOD	CANS	NAGS	CANOE	DEACONS

46

128

Don't Coat Me On This

The answer to this joke is written using a simple code.

First, circle each letter that's immediately to the right of a W. We did the first one to get you started. Then write the circled letters (starting at the top and reading left to right) in the spaces below to answer this joke:

What coat is always wet when you put it on?

R M Z G V M O T J W Ⓐ B

W Ⓒ N I Q U N Z U X Y U

B Q W Ⓞ T U X O V E E E

I G B W Ⓐ H Q E S M E X

K M I Q L J W Ⓣ X S Z A

Z Q E N B W Ⓞ P Z B M I

X M W Ⓕ Q E N R V I Z R

W Ⓟ Z M R U Y Q M S K S

B U X D O U M R K Q W Ⓐ

J F V R Q L I O W Ⓘ K J

B S W Ⓝ I X S R D Q R K

W Ⓣ Q S L Z M G E D O Y

Write the circled letters here:

A COAT OF PAINT

47

Dog and Fox Trot

Which one of these drawings is exactly the same as the ORIGINAL?
Look carefully and circle the one that is exactly the same.

ORIGINAL

1

2

3

4

5

Frank Firster

Use the clues to write one letter in each square. We did the first one to get
you started. We also included the alphabet at the bottom to help with some
of the clues. When you're done, read across to find the answer to this joke:

What did the hot dog say when it won the race?

The first word:

1. The letter that's another word for ME
2. The repeated letter in MUMMY

The second word:

3. The middle letter of SIGNATURE

The third word:

4. The letter that looks like an upside-down M
5. The letter between H and J
6. The 1st letter when you spell out the number 8
7. The letter that's in both SONG and DANCE
8. The 5th letter of the alphabet
9. The 6th letter of UNIVERSE

I ' M

A

W I E N E R !

ABCDEFGHIJKLMNOPQRSTUVWXYZ

Food's On!

Find and circle the 20 words
listed below. The hidden words can
read forward, backward, up, down,
and diagonally in all directions.

| M J Y E W J J H A P K U |
| G Y N E K C I H C A H S |
| N O C A B S G G E N B E |
| U I O T A M O T R C U I |
| R M F R I E S O E A R L |
| C C H L T J A A A K G G |
| B T K E U Q N S L E E G |
| G R E N N I D T V S R B |
| I O V S A H W Y D A R P |
| U L O F R U I T V L P V |
| U L O T Q S C Y J A I U |
| N S T W V N H P R D X B |

EGGS	BACON	LUNCH	TOAST	TOMATO
MILK	FRIES	ROLLS	BURGER	CHICKEN
RICE	FRUIT	SALAD	CEREAL	PANCAKES
TUNA	GRAVY	STEAK	DINNER	SANDWICH

In Apple Pie Order

There are seven questions on the left, and seven joke answers on the right.
Match them up by writing the correct number in each space.

What did
the apple say
to the orange?   A. 4

Who led
the apples to
the bakery?   B. 3

When
is an apple
grouchy?   C. 7

If an apple a
day keeps the doctor
away, what does an
onion do?   D. 1

What
kind of fruit do
you get if you cross
Christmas trees with
apple trees?   E. 2

What's the best
thing to put into an
apple pie?   F. 5

What do you call
apples with bees in
front of them?   G. 6

1. Keeps
everyone away.

2. Pineapples.

3. The
pie piper.

4. Nothing,
apples can't
talk.

5. Your teeth.

6. Bapples.

7. When
it's a crab
apple.

Loco Motive

Put the 14 words into the grid
in alphabetical order. We did the first
one to get you started. Then write the
highlighted letters from top to bottom
in the spaces below to answer this joke:

How does a train eat?

RHYME

CRATE

DIGIT

HATCH

OCEAN

MEOWS

ITCHY

GUSTY

FIEND

BRAIN

SERVE

TWIST

EVOKE

LEVEL

Write the highlighted letters here:

I T   G O E S

C H E W   C H E W

B	R	A	I	N
C	R	A	T	E
D	I	G	I	T
E	V	O	K	E
F	I	E	N	D
G	U	S	T	Y
H	A	T	C	H
I	T	C	H	Y
L	E	V	E	L
M	E	O	W	S
O	C	E	A	N
R	H	Y	M	E
S	E	R	V	E
T	W	I	S	T

Kick Ball

Cross off every letter that appears MORE THAN TWICE in the grid.
Then write the leftover letters (starting at the top and reading left to right)
in the spaces below to find the answer to this question:

What direction should you kick a ball
if you want to easily get it back?

X X B X S X X X X

X X W T B R X X X

X X X X A X X W X

X X I X X G X X

X X X H X X X X

X T X X X X X X

X X X U X X X X

X X X X X P X X

Write the leftover letters here:

S T R A I G H T   U P

Elf Portrait

Which one of these drawings is exactly the same as the ORIGINAL?
Look carefully and circle the one that is exactly the same.

ORIGINAL

1

2

3

4

5

54

Fang You Very Much

The answer to this joke is written using a simple code.

First, circle each letter that's immediately to the right of an F.
We did the first one to get you started. Then write the
circled letters (starting at the top and reading left to right)
in the spaces below to answer this joke.

What part of the street do vampires live on?

```
T  R  X  D  F (T) V  E  N  R  Q  W
P  H  R  W  K  J  F (H) Y  V  N  G
E  O  U  J  F (E) W  V  N  N  I  Q
U  N  Z  U  X  Y  U  B  Q  N  V  I
U  D  O  B  C  F (D) I  G  C  Z  E
H  Q  E  F (E) M  E  M  E  A  Q  L
J  F (A) X  S  Z  A  Q  W  A  S  Y
Z  Q  E  N  V  B  L  P  F (D) M  I
B  S  M  N  I  X  S  R  D  Q  V  A
V  L  Q  S  L  Z  F (E) E  D  O  Y
X  F (N) V  L  E  N  R  P  I  Z  R
G  X  Z  M  R  U  Y  Q  M  V  F (D)
```

Write the circled letters here:

T H E   D E A D   E N D

55

Hyperbole

Hyperbole (HI-PER-BOWL-EE) is exaggerated talk, such as saying,
"That ice cream cone is a mile high and the best one in the entire world!"

Your job is to write down as many words as possible using just the letters in
HYPERBOLE. No proper nouns and at least THREE letters long. OK, go!

HERE'S OUR LIST OF COMMON WORDS
If you think of others that are in the dictionary, count them!

BEE	PEE	HERO	RELY
BOP	PER	HOLE	ROBE
BOY	PLY	HOLY	ROLE
BYE	PRO	HOPE	ROPE
EEL	PRY	LOBE	YELP
EYE	ROB	LOPE	ELOPE
HER	RYE	LORE	PROBE
HEY	YEP	OBEY	REBEL
HOE	BEEP	PEEL	REPEL
HOP	BEER	PEER	REPLY
LOB	BORE	PLOY	HELPER
LOP	HEEL	POLE	HEREBY
LYE	HELP	PORE	
ORB	HERB	PREY	
ORE	HERE	REEL	

56

In the Neighborhood

Find and circle the 20 words
listed below. The hidden words can
read forward, backward, up, down,
and diagonally in all directions.

```
X  S  E  W  E  R  E  B  N  C  S  E
S  J  C  Y  O  C  Z  V  X  R  G  S
E  X  L  A  N  E  Q  C  B  C  P  M
S  I  D  E  W  A  L  K  V  U  I  P
U  L  F  N  G  D  E  H  S  R  S  F
O  Q  H  M  C  A  M  N  S  B  T  H
H  J  L  X  B  S  R  W  A  X  O  N
W  H  B  D  C  T  K  A  R  A  O  A
T  Q  J  L  U  M  J  G  C  P  Y
B  G  K  K  O  Y  E  L  L  A  A  Y
E  P  Q  M  K  C  T  E  E  R  T  S
C  P  S  B  G  M  K  I  D  S  H  E
```

CAR	KIDS	SHED	FENCE	STOOP
BUSH	LAWN	YARD	GRASS	GARAGE
CURB	PATH	ALLEY	HOUSE	STREET
GATE	ROAD	BLOCK	SEWER	SIDEWALK

57

Let's Be Frank

Cross off every letter that appears MORE THAN TWICE in the grid.
Then write the leftover letters (starting at the top and reading left to right)
in the spaces below to find the answer to this question:

How do you make
a hot dog stand?

```
X  S  X  X  X  X  G  X
X  X  T  X  X  E  X  X
X  X  M  A  X  X  X  L
X  X  X  G  I  X  X  X
X  T  X  X  X  S  X  X
X  X  X  C  X  X  X  X
H  X  X  X  X  A  X
X  X  I  X  X  X  R  X
```

Write the leftover letters here:

S T E A L   I T S   C H A I R

58

Fruit Feet

Use the clues to write one letter in each square. We did the first one to get
you started. We also included the alphabet at the bottom to help with some
of the clues. When you're done, read across to find the answer to this joke:

Who makes shoes for fruit?

The first word:

1. The letter that comes after O
2. The letter that has three straight lines pointing to the right
3. The letter that's farthest from Z
4. The letter that sounds like SEA
5. The letter that starts with an A sound (but it's not the letter A)

The second word:

6. The middle letter of APPLICATION
7. The most common letter in FOOTNOTE
8. The letter that comes 10 letters before L
9. The letter that comes 9 letters before K
10. The 5th letter in FAMILY
11. The letter that's repeated in EAGLE
12. The letter that isn't repeated in STREETS
13. The last letter of most plural words

P E A C H
C O B B L E R S

ABCDEFGHIJKLMNOPQRSTUVWXYZ

59

May the Sweets Be With You

Put the 10 words into the grid in alphabetical order. We did the first one to get you started. Then write the highlighted letters from top to bottom in the spaces below to answer this joke:

What is a Jedi Knight's favorite candy?

WHEEL
SCRAM
EMAIL
CLAIM
MUFFS
PRISM
DEALT
OCTET
YEARN
VALVE

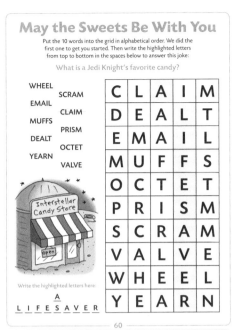

C	L	A	I	M
D	E	A	L	T
E	M	A	I	L
M	U	F	F	S
O	C	T	E	T
P	R	I	S	M
S	C	R	A	M
V	A	L	V	E
W	H	E	E	L
Y	E	A	R	N

Write the highlighted letters here:

A L I F E S A V E R

Mr. Puss

Starting at Mr. Puss, follow the different pieces of yarn to find out which one leads to the yarn ball.

I Spy

Use the word and picture clues to fill in the answers, one letter per square.

If you don't know an answer, try filling in ones nearby or that go in the opposite direction.

ACROSS
1 ___ Vegas, Nevada
4 How old you are is your ___
5 Bugs Bunny line: "What's up, ___?" (also a short word for a medical person)
6 Word in a cheerleader's cheer
9 What you see with
10 "And they lived happily ever ___"
12 Vegetable used to make a thick green soup
13 Type of leg for a pirate (it's wooden)
14 What you hear with
17 Pen point
18 Letters added in front of "cycle" that makes it a three-wheeler

DOWN
1 Young boy
2 "How long ___ did you get here?"
3 Undercover spy (2 words)
7 "Yes," aboard a pirate ship
8 Opposite of "him"
10 A 99¢ game added on to a smartphone, for example
11 Admission price, or a doctor's charge
15 The stuff you breathe
16 Baseball abbreviation for "runs batted in"

Looking for a Lake

Cross off every letter that appears MORE THAN TWICE in the grid. Then write the leftover letters (starting at the top and reading left to right) in the spaces below to find the answer to this question:

What state is Lake Tahoe in?

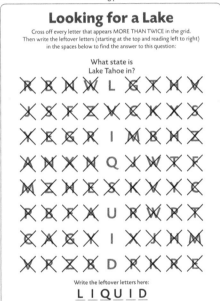

Write the leftover letters here:

L I Q U I D

Having a Beach Ball

Which one of these drawings is exactly the same as the ORIGINAL? Look carefully and circle the one that is exactly the same.

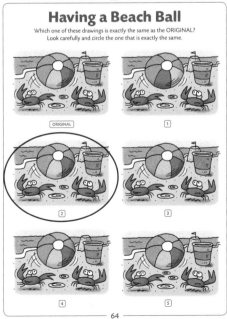

131

Outstanding in His Field

Use the clues to write one letter in each square. We did the first one to get you started. We also included the alphabet at the bottom to help with some of the clues. When you're done, read across to find the answer to this joke:

What did Baby Corn ask Mom Corn?

The first word:

1. The letter before X
2. The letter between G and I
3. The letter that's repeated in EEK
4. The letter that sounds like the verb in YOU ARE HERE
5. The most common letter in TEMPERATURE

The second word:

6. The middle letter of CAPITAL
7. The beginning or end of SNAKES

The third word:

8. The letter that sounds like a little, round, green vegetable
9. The letter that sounds like OH
10. The letter that's repeated in PURPLE
11. The letter that appears once in ONCE but never in ONE
12. The letter that appears in DOUBLE or NOTHING
13. The letter that's 5 letters before the T in RABBIT
14. The middle letter of EXPLANATION

W H E R E
I S
P O P C O R N ?

ABCDEFGHIJKLMNOPQRSTUVWXYZ

Stationary Bike

Cross off every letter that appears MORE THAN TWICE in the grid.
Then write the leftover letters (starting at the top and reading left to right)
in the spaces below to find the answer to this question:

**Why wouldn't the
bike go any farther?**

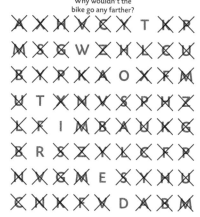

Write the leftover letters here:

IT WAS <u>TWO TIRED</u>

66

WAIT!

Don't read any further if you haven't
looked at the page BEFORE this one.

Monster Mash

OK, now let's see what you remember.

Write your answers in the blanks
after each question.

1. How many ghosts are there in the wooden tub? <u>three</u>
2. What is the name of the big, purple, globby monster? <u>Jerry</u>
3. There's a green octopus-like tentacle in the upper left. What is it doing?
   <u>It's roasting a marshmallow over a flame from the torch</u>
4. Are any of the monsters wearing hats? YES or NO <u>NO</u>
5. What is the vat number on the wooden tub? <u>14</u>
6. What is the number of snakes listed on the sign on the side of the crate? <u>15</u>
7. How many snakes can you see IN the crate? <u>five</u>
8. How many snakes can you see OUTSIDE the crate? <u>one</u>
9. What is the crocodile in the lower right doing? <u>sleeping</u>
10. What kind of cereal is in the box? <u>rat</u>

68

La La Land

There are seven questions on the left, and seven joke answers on the right.
Match them up by writing the correct number in each space.

Why wouldn't the piano play any music? — A. <u>3</u>

What makes music on your hair? — B. <u>1</u>

Why are pirates great singers? — C. <u>7</u>

What rock group has four guys who don't sing? — D. <u>2</u>

What is a cat's favorite song? — E. <u>6</u>

What has forty feet and sings? — F. <u>4</u>

What is a vampire's favorite part of the guitar? — G. <u>5</u>

1. A Head Band.
2. Mount Rushmore.
3. It lost its keys.
4. A school choir.
5. The neck.
6. Three Blind Mice.
7. They're always hitting the high C's.

69

It's Magic!

Find and circle the 20 words
listed below. The hidden words can
read forward, backward, up, down,
and diagonally in all directions.

S	F	Q	X	T	D	Q	N	M	D	N	T
F	D	N	J	P	W	R	F	N	Z	R	O
C	L	I	W	B	L	T	A	L	E	O	Z
B	H	L	A	T	E	W	B	G	D	C	F
F	C	B	R	M	P	F	L	S	O	I	C
A	F	T	O	S	O	R	C	E	R	Y	N
A	I	G	Z	O	E	E	L	F	S	U	P
F	W	B	G	R	C	Y	M	L	A	O	R
W	E	A	S	N	K	H	A	R	Y	T	I
E	A	S	N	K	H	A	R	Y	T	I	T
E	R	G	O	J	A	Q	X	I	N	B	E
H	T	E	M	P	U	S	O	N	A	P	E
Y	S	K	E	S	N	N	V	G	F	F	B

ELF	WAND	WARTS	GOBLIN	MERMAID
FROG	FABLE	WITCH	POTION	SORCERY
OGRE	FAIRY	DRAGON	SPRITE	UNICORN
TALE	GNOME	FLYING	FANTASY	LEPRECHAUN

70

Polar Exploration

Which penguin chick belongs to which parent?
Follow the tangled lines to find out. Then write the
correct letter on the line below the parent's number.

71

X Marks the Spot

Use the word and picture clues to
fill in the answers, one letter per square.

If you don't know an answer, try filling in ones
nearby or that go in the opposite direction.

1-Down

ACROSS
1 2,000 pounds
4 Stroke, as a dog's belly
5 Period of history (when spelled backwards, it's the plural of "is")
6 Salty body of water
8 Sounds people make when they get hurt
9 Dr. ___ (author of *The Cat in the Hat*)
12 Style of music that's features a strong beat and spoken rhyme
13 Abbr. for "expected time of arrival," such as when a flight is due
14 Short word for mother
16 Word of discovery when cracking a case
17 Smallish spoon measurement (abbr.)

DOWN
1 Paper marked with an X to show where a valuable chest is buried (2 words)
2 "It'll be ___ secret" (yours and my)
3 Org. for basketball teams like the Knicks and the Lakers (abbreviation)
6 Letters meaning "help!" when a ship is sinking
7 Female sheep
10 Used a chair or bench
10 Relaxing place to go (maybe even get a mud bath)
14 "Welcome" might be printed on it below the front door
15 Surprised sounds

Crossword grid:
T O N
R U B
E R A
S E A
O W S
S E U S S
R A P
E T A
M O M
A H A
T S P

2000 LBS (1-Across) · 7-Down · 14-Down (Welcome)

72

132

On the Road

Fill in the boxes in the BLANK GRID by copying exactly what you see in the same-numbered boxes in the SCRAMBLED GRID.

SCRAMBLED GRID

BLANK GRID

Jokesmith

A smith is someone who makes something.
So a jokesmith is someone who makes jokes. Simple, right?

Your job is to write down as many words as possible using just the letters in JOKESMITH. No proper nouns and at least THREE letters long. OK, go!

HERE'S OUR LIST OF COMMON WORDS
If you think of others that are in the dictionary, count them!

HEM	THE	JOKE	SHOT	JOIST
HIM	TIE	JOTS	SITE	JOKES
HIS	TOE	KITE	SKIM	KITES
HIT	TOM	KITS	SKIT	MITES
HOE	EMIT	MESH	SOME	MOIST
HOT	HEMS	METS	STEM	OMITS
ITS	HIKE	MIKE	THEM	SHEIK
JET	HITS	MIST	THIS	SMITH
JOE	HOES	MITE	TIES	SMOKE
JOT	HOME	MOST	TIME	SMOTE
KIT	HOSE	MOTE	TOES	STOKE
MET	HOST	MOTH	EMITS	THOSE
SET	ITEM	OMIT	HIKES	TIMES
SHE	JEST	SEMI	HOIST	
SIT	JETS	SHIM	HOMES	
SKI	JOES	SHOE	ITEMS	

On the Beach

Find and circle the 20 words listed below. The hidden words can read forward, backward, up, down, and diagonally in all directions.

CRAB	PIER	COAST	WATER	UMBRELLA
FISH	SAND	DUNES	WAVES	BEACHBALL
GULL	TIDE	SHARK	SHOVEL	BOARDWALK
PAIL	CHAIR	TOWEL	FRISBEE	SUNGLASSES

On the Moon

Which one of these drawings is exactly the same as the ORIGINAL?
Look carefully and circle the one that is exactly the same.

Science...Not!

Use the clues to write one letter in each square. We did the first one to get you started. We also included the alphabet at the bottom to help with some of the clues. When you're done, read across to find the answer to this joke:

How do you make antifreeze?

The first word:
1. The 1st letter in SCIENCE
2. The letter that sounds like a little peg you put a golfball on
3. The most common letter in ENVELOPE
4. The middle letter in OPERATION
5. The 12th letter of the alphabet

The second word:
6. The last letter in TRASH
7. The vowel that's repeated in LETTER
8. The letter that's 4 letters after N

The third word:
9. The most common letter in BUBBLEGUM
10. The letter that looks like the left side and bottom of a rectangle
11. The 7th letter of INFORMATION
12. The letter that's in NOW and AGAIN
13. The letter that's in TRUNK but not RUNT
14. The 2nd vowel alphabetically
15. The letter that starts TROUBLE

S	T	E	A	L

H	E	R

B	L	A	N	K	E	T

ABCDEFGHIJKLMNOPQRSTUVWXYZ

Show Me the Money

There are seven questions on the left, and seven joke answers on the right.
Match them up by writing the correct number in each space.

Where do fish keep their money? A. 6

How do dinosaurs pay their bills? B. 3

Why did the crook shower before robbing a bank? C. 5

What has two heads and two tails but no arms or legs? D. 2

What kind of money do crabs use? E. 1

Why is a football game worth a dollar? F. 7

Why is a nickel smarter than a penny? G. 4

1. Sand dollars.
2. Two pennies.
3. With Tyrannosaurus checks.
4. It has more cents.
5. He wanted to make a clean getaway.
6. In river banks.
7. It has four quarters.

133

On the Farm

Find and circle the 20 words listed below. The hidden words can read forward, backward, up, down, and diagonally in all directions.

```
M U J F V G X A P Y H X
A G T N Z Z N E P A G T
W B A R N E K C I H C D
S I L O N I A R G O X F
W O R C E R A C S W O C
D O Z P D T M E H O R E
B G L F D R L A E B C K
B O F P K A T D E B H V
H D O K B C E F P M A D
G E M M F T W R O N R K
N A A Q J O F I E L D M
O G U H O R S E E D S U
```

HAY	COWS	SILO	GRAIN	CHICKEN
PEN	LOFT	VANE	HORSE	ORCHARD
BARN	PIGS	BALES	SEEDS	TRACTOR
CORN	PLOW	FIELD	SHEEP	SCARECROW

Stay Awake!

Cross off every letter that appears MORE THAN TWICE in the grid. Then write the leftover letters (starting at the top and reading left to right) in the spaces below to find the answer to this question:

How can you go eight days without sleep?

Write the leftover letters here:

<u>S L E E P</u> <u>A T</u> <u>N I G H T</u>

Termite Time

The answer to this joke is written using a simple code.

First, circle each letter that's immediately to the right of a D. We did the first one to get you started. Then write the circled letters (starting at the top and reading left to right) in the spaces below to answer this joke:

What do termites eat for dessert?

```
R Q D T T U X O V C E W
I G C Z M H Q E S M E X
E M I Q L D O K X S Z A
D O X P O U M R K Q O B
G F D T Q W I O R W K J
Z Q E N B O L P Z B M I
B S M N I X D H F Q R K
A D P S L Z M G E C O Y
L M E E Q E N R V I D I
G X Z M R D C Q M S K S
O Y D K V M O U J B F W
A M N I Q U N Z U D S U
```

Write the circled letters here:

<u>T O O T H P I C K S</u>

Petty Party

Which one of these drawings is exactly the same as the ORIGINAL? Look carefully and circle the one that is exactly the same.

ORIGINAL

1   2   3   4   5

Peabrain

Peabrain is what you might call someone who isn't too smart. But you're a very polite person — we can tell — so it's unlikely you've ever used such a word.

Your job is to write down as many words as possible using just the letters in PEABRAIN. No proper nouns and at least THREE letters long. OK, go!

HERE'S OUR LIST OF COMMON WORDS
If you think of others that are in the dictionary, count them!

AIR	NIP	AREA	PARE
APE	PAN	ARIA	PEAR
ARE	PAR	BANE	PIER
BAN	PEA	BARE	PINE
BAR	PEN	BARN	RAIN
BIN	PER	BEAN	REAP
BRA	PIE	BEAR	REIN
EAR	PIN	BRAN	RIPE
ERA	RAN	EARN	ARENA
IRE	RAP	NEAR	BRAIN
NAB	REP	PAIN	BRINE
NAP	RIB	PAIR	RIPEN
NIB	RIP	PANE	

Sick as a Dog

Use the clues to write one letter in each square. We did the first one to get you started. We also included the alphabet at the bottom to help with some of the clues. When you're done, read across to find the answer to this joke:

What does a sick dog say?

The first word:

1. The 2nd letter of the alphabet
2. The letter made by adding a line to an upside-down V
3. The middle letter of AMPERSAND (that's the word for this: &)
4. The most common letter in OFFICE

The second word:

5. The letter that sounds like a buzzing insect
6. The letter that's repeated in ALPHABET
7. The letter that sounds like the verb ARE
8. The 6th letter of the alphabet

The third word:

9. The middle letter in the word PROBLEM
10. The letter that comes nine letters before J
11. The letter between Q and S
12. The letter that appears in both FORE and A

1 B	2 A	3 R	4 F
5 B	6 A	7 R	8 F
9 B	10 A	11 R	12 F

ABCDEFGHIJKLMNOPQRSTUVWXYZ

Monster Match

Put the 14 words into the grid in alphabetical order. We did the first one to get you started. Then write the highlighted letters from top to bottom in the spaces below to answer this joke:

Who did Frankenstein's monster bring to the dance?

JOUST
LOFTY
NERVE
YODEL
KILNS
ALOHA
PRESS
SANDY
BRAID
ETHER
CRASH
OLIVE
IVORY
DIGIT

A	L	O	H	A
B	R	A	I	D
C	R	A	S	H
D	I	G	I	T
E	T	H	E	R
I	V	O	R	Y
J	O	U	S	T
K	I	L	N	S
L	O	F	T	Y
N	E	R	V	E
O	L	I	V	E
P	R	E	S	S
S	A	N	D	Y
Y	O	D	E	L

Write the highlighted letters here: H I S G H O U L F R I E N D

85

Sports!

Find and circle the 20 words listed below. The hidden words can read forward, backward, up, down, and diagonally in all directions.

S	Q	U	A	S	H	V	H	A	W	U	D
I	E	L	O	Y	B	G	U	R	C	R	V
N	H	U	T	L	N	R	E	C	C	O	S
N	F	V	V	P	O	S	E	H	R	W	U
E	L	T	L	K	T	P	G	E	R	I	M
T	O	H	G	L	N	N	G	R	Y	N	O
A	G	A	R	A	D	G	N	Y	K	G	I
R	F	N	A	F	M	C	I	Z	E	T	B
A	G	I	R	C	D	V	C	L	T	N	I
K	J	U	D	O	A	D	N	H	H	X	H
P	S	L	L	A	B	Y	E	L	L	O	V
G	Y	E	O	U	D	C	F	Y	H	B	Y

GOLF   CANOE   KARATE   TENNIS   SURFING
JUDO   RUGBY   ROWING   ARCHERY   BADMINTON
POLO   BOXING   SOCCER   CRICKET   WRESTLING
SUMO   DIVING   SQUASH   FENCING   VOLLEYBALL

86

Out of School

Fill in the boxes in the BLANK GRID by copying exactly what you see in the same-numbered boxes in the SCRAMBLED GRID.

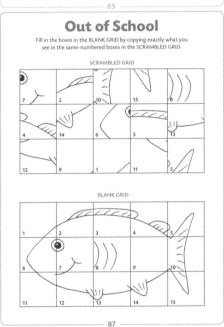

SCRAMBLED GRID

BLANK GRID

87

Moon Munchies

Put the 11 words into the grid in alphabetical order. We did the first one to get you started. Then write the highlighted letters from top to bottom in the spaces below to answer this joke:

How do you know when the moon has had enough to eat?

STALK
DEMON
HITCH
ENTER
CHIMP
AWAKE
QUAFF
ROGUE
JESTS
VAULT
GRIND

A	W	A	K	E
C	H	I	M	P
D	E	M	O	N
E	N	T	E	R
G	R	I	N	D
H	I	T	C	H
J	E	S	T	S
Q	U	A	F	F
R	O	G	U	E
S	T	A	L	K
V	A	U	L	T

Write the highlighted letters here:
W H E N I T ' S
F U L L

88

Moon Meeting

There are 10 differences between the moonscape on this page and the one on the next page. Can you find and circle all 10 of them?

91

135

What's the Dif'?

The answer to this joke is written using a simple code.

First, circle each letter that's immediately to the right of a B. We did the first one to get you started. Then write the circled letters (starting at the top and reading left to right) in the spaces below to answer this joke:

What's the difference between here and there?

O	B	T	G	V	M	O	U	J	M	F	W
A	M	N	B	H	U	N	Z	U	X	Y	U
T	Q	N	M	B	E	X	O	V	C	E	W
I	G	C	Z	M	H	Q	E	S	M	E	X
E	M	B	L	L	J	U	K	X	S	Z	A
R	U	X	D	O	B	E	R	K	Q	O	R
M	F	V	R	Q	W	B	T	R	W	K	J
Z	Q	E	N	C	O	L	P	Z	B	T	I
O	S	M	B	E	X	S	R	D	Q	R	K
A	B	R	S	L	Z	M	G	E	D	O	Y
X	M	E	E	Q	E	N	R	V	I	Z	R
G	X	Z	M	B	T	Y	Q	M	S	K	S

Write the circled letters here:
T H E L E T T E R T

92

Root for Trees

There are seven questions on the left, and seven joke answers on the right.
Match them up by writing the correct number in each space.

What kind of tree can fit in your hand? — A. **3**

What did the trees wear to the beach? — B. **7**

What did the beaver say to the tree? — C. **1**

What did the little tree say to the big bully tree? — D. **6**

What kind of tree has the most friends? — E. **5**

What is the tastiest kind of tree? — F. **4**

How do you identify a dogwood tree? — G. **2**

1. Nice gnawing you.
2. By its bark.
3. A palm tree.
4. A pastry.
5. Poplar.
6. Leaf me alone.
7. Swimming trunks.

93

Start Walking

Use the clues to write one letter in each square. We did the first one to get
you started. We also included the alphabet at the bottom to help with some
of the clues. When you're done, read across to find the answer to this joke:

Where do you send a shoe in the summer?

The first word:

1. The letter before C
2. The letter that looks like a zero
3. The letter repeated in BOOK
4. The letter that is halfway between O and Y

The second word:

5. The middle letter of PRINCIPAL
6. The letter that's the best grade on a homework assignment
7. The letter that looks like an upside-down W
8. The letter that's repeated in PUMPING

B O O T
C A M P

ABCDEFGHIJKLMNOPQRSTUVWXYZ

94

School Time

There are seven questions on the left, and seven joke answers on the right.
Match them up by writing the correct number in each space.

What's the worst thing about a school cafeteria? — A. **4**

How do you get straight A's? — B. **6**

What do elves learn in school? — C. **1**

When do you eat at astronaut school? — D. **5**

Why were the teacher's eyes crossed? — E. **7**

What do you do if a teacher rolls her eyes at you? — F. **2**

Why did the teacher write instructions on the window? — G. **3**

1. The elf-abet.
2. Pick them up and roll them back.
3. So they would be clear.
4. The food.
5. At launch time.
6. Draw them with a ruler.
7. She couldn't control her pupils.

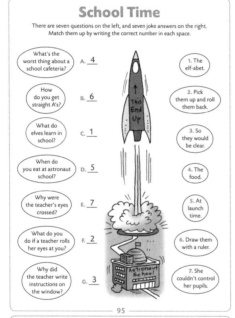

95

Pool Cat

Put the 10 words into the grid in alphabetical order. We did the
first one to get you started. Then write the highlighted letters
from top to bottom in the spaces below to answer this joke:

What kind of cat likes the water?

GECKO
NIPPY
LATCH
CRANE
BREAK
TASTY
FLOOR
PLUSH
RESET
MOODY

B R E A K
C R A N E
F L O O R
G E C K O
L A T C H
M O O D Y
N I P P Y
P L U S H
R E S E T
T A S T Y

Write the highlighted letters here:
A N
O C T O - P U S S

96

Rib-Tickler

A rib-tickler is a funny joke. One that's so funny it gets inside you and
tickles your ribs. It might require a sidesplitting joke to get in there.

Your job is to write down as many words as possible using just the letters in
RIB-TICKLER. No proper nouns and at least THREE letters long. OK, go!

HERE'S OUR LIST OF COMMON WORDS
If you think of others that are in the dictionary, count them!

BET	TIE	RICE	LITER
BIT	TIL	RITE	RELIC
ELK	BELT	TICK	TRIBE
ERR	BIKE	TIER	TRICK
ICE	BILE	TILE	TRIER
ILK	BILK	TIRE	BICKER
IRE	BITE	TREK	ELICIT
IRK	CITE	BIKER	TICKER
KIT	CRIB	BITER	TICKLE
LET	KILT	BRICK	TRICKLE
LIE	KITE	BRIER	TRICKIER
LIT	LICE	CLERK	
RIB	LICK	CRIER	
TIC	LIKE	ICIER	

97

Whazzit?

The answer to this joke is written using a simple code.

First, circle each letter that's immediately to the right of an L.
We did the first one to get you started. Then write the
circled letters (starting at the top and reading left to right)
in the spaces below to answer this joke:

What has four wheels and flies?

A Q W A R O Z Q E L (A) B
L (G) F D M I B V M N I X
K R D Q V A V P L (A) O Z
F E L (R) O Y X F N V M E
N R P I T L (B) D F T V E
N R L (A) W P H R W L (G) F
H S E N L (E) O U J F E W
V L (T) T Q U N Z U X Y U
B Q N V S U D L (R) C F D
I G C Z E H Q E F E L (U)
E L (C) Q T J F A X B P Z
R G L (K) M R U Y Q M V F

Write the circled letters here:

A **G A R B A G E** **T R U C K**

98

Running Home

Put the 10 words into the grid in alphabetical order. We did the first one to get you started. Then write the highlighted letters from top to bottom in the spaces below to answer this joke:

Which baseball players leave almost as soon as they arrive?

UPSET
HURRY
FRONT
INTRO
TEPEE
JESTS
ETHER
MATCH
~~AISLE~~
OZONE

A	I	S	L	E
E	T	H	E	R
F	R	O	N	T
H	U	R	R	Y
I	N	T	R	O
J	E	S	T	S
M	A	T	C	H
O	Z	O	N	E
T	E	P	E	E
U	P	S	E	T

Hey, I gotta go.

Write the highlighted letters here: S H O R T S T O P S

100

Snow People

Which one of these drawings is exactly the same as the ORIGINAL? Look carefully and circle the one that is exactly the same.

ORIGINAL
1
2
3
4
5

101

Too Cool for School

Find and circle the 20 words listed below. The hidden words can read forward, backward, up, down, and diagonally in all directions.

F	E	F	R	E	H	C	A	E	T	A	V
Y	D	K	P	H	W	I	C	M	P	N	W
D	A	E	R	E	I	N	S	K	R	N	X
U	R	U	I	O	E	B	K	T	O	T	Y
T	G	C	N	I	W	J	M	S	O	L	W
S	C	I	C	G	P	E	S	Q	M	R	S
W	Q	S	I	O	V	E	M	A	Q	H	Y
M	P	U	P	I	L	S	K	O	O	B	D
E	W	M	A	T	H	L	S	V	H	D	Z
B	M	Y	L	R	B	G	E	A	H	W	P
I	W	G	A	H	T	T	D	G	L	L	A
R	X	J	H	S	I	L	G	N	E	C	X

ART	MATH	GRADE	LESSON	SCIENCE
GYM	READ	MUSIC	COLLEGE	TEACHER
BOOK	ROOM	PUPIL	ENGLISH	HOMEWORK
DESK	CLASS	STUDY	HISTORY	PRINCIPAL

102

Smellfungus

A smellfungus is a person who finds fault with everything – you know, like someone who thinks everything smells like fungus!

Your job is to write down as many words as possible using just the letters in SMELLFUNGUS No proper nouns and at least THREE letters long. OK, go!

HERE'S OUR LIST OF COMMON WORDS
If you think of others that are in the dictionary, count them!

ELF	ELMS	GUNS	SLUM	LUNGS
ELM	EMUS	LEGS	SMUG	MENUS
EMU	FELL	LENS	SNUG	MULES
FLU	FLUE	LESS	SUES	MUSES
FUN	FUEL	LUGE	SUMS	SELLS
GEL	FULL	LULU	SUNG	SLUGS
GEM	FUME	LUNG	SUNS	SLUMS
GNU	FUSE	MENS	USES	SLUNG
GUM	FUSS	MENU	FLUNG	SMELL
GUN	GELS	MESS	FUELS	ENGULF
LEG	GEMS	MUGS	FUMES	FUNGUS
LUG	GLEN	MULE	FUSES	MUSSEL
MEN	GLUE	MULL	GLENS	SMELLS
MUG	GLUM	MUSE	GLUES	SULLEN
SUE	GNUS	NULL	GUESS	UNLESS
SUM	GULF	SELF	GULFS	USEFUL
SUN	GULL	SELL	GULLS	ENGULFS
USE	GUMS	SLUG	LUNGE	FULLNESS

103

So Long, Soccer

There are seven questions on the left, and seven joke answers on the right. Match them up by writing the correct number in each space.

Where's the best place to buy a soccer uniform? A. 2

What's a ghost's favorite soccer position? B. 4

Why is Cinderella a lousy soccer player? C. 5

What do grasshoppers like to watch more than soccer? D. 7

How do soccer players stay cool during games? E. 1

What runs around a soccer field but never moves? F. 3

Why was the soccer field wet after the game? G. 6

1. They stand near the fans.
2. New Jersey.
3. A fence.
4. Ghoul keeper.
5. She always runs away from the ball.
6. The players dribbled all over it.
7. Cricket.

104

What's the Connection?

Use the clues to write one letter in each square. We did the first one to get you started. We also included the alphabet at the bottom to help with some of the clues. When you're done, read across to find the answer to this joke:

What do Alexander the Great and Kermit the Frog have in common?

The first word:
1. The middle letter of ASK
2. The letter that comes 5 letters before F
3. The letter that's in TAME but not EAT
4. The letter that's repeated in SQUEEZE

The second word:
5. The letter that's both before and after an E in CEMENT
6. The repeated letter in INITIAL
7. The last letter of GROUND
8. The 4th letter of the alphabet
9. The letter in AIL that's not a vowel
10. The letter in STRENGTH that is a vowel

The third word:
11. The letter that comes 3 letters before Q
12. The letter that's in ANGRIEST but not STINGER
13. The letter between L and N
14. The middle letter in DANDELION

S	A	M	E
M	I	D	D	L	E
N	A	M	E

ABCDEFGHIJKLMNOPQRSTUVWXYZ

105

137

You Can Lick 'Em

Use the word and picture clues to
fill in the answers, one letter per square.

If you don't know an answer, try filling in ones
nearby or that go in the opposite direction.

ACROSS

1 Green, clinging plant that can grow on buildings
4 How the third letter of the alphabet could be spelled out
5 People who write things like "Violets are blue, I love you"
7 Curved path a softball follows after being hit
8 Body part that feels pain (such as in a tooth)
11 One that sticks out on either side of the head
12 Denim pants
14 Limb that's inside a sleeve
15 Crazy or goofy
18 Part used to row a canoe
19 Camping structures used for sleeping
21 Cheer at a bullfight
22 Gives an approval

DOWN

1 They're made of a scoop or many piled on top of each other
2 Dog or cat doctor, for short
3 The opposite of "no"
5 An egg is fried in it on a stove
6 Gold, silver, or iron is a type of this valuable rock
9 Big moving truck
10 Hospital areas where people go for emergency treatment (for short)
12 Bony part of your head that contains your chin and teeth
13 Important time period
16 Kit-___ candy bar
17 365-day periods (abbreviation)
19 Also
20 Antlered animal that's in between a deer and a moose in size

Grid answers: IVY, CEE, POETS, ARC, NERVE, EAR, JEANS, ARM, WACKY, OAR, TENTS, OLE, OKS

R-I-G-H-T

The right way to solve this maze is to spell RIGHT!
It may look easy, but there's only one way to do it.

You have to be sharp to solve this!

Ohh.

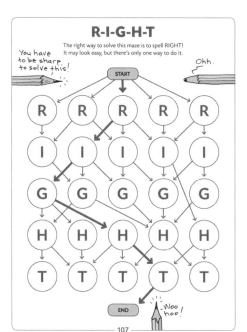

START

R R R R R
I I I I I
G G G G G
H H H H H
T T T T T

END

Woo hoo!

Wild and Woolly

The answer to this joke is written using a simple code.

First, circle each letter that's immediately to the right of an S.
We did the first one to get you started. Then write the
circled letters (starting at the top and reading left to right)
in the spaces below to answer this joke:

BAA BAA

Where do sheep watch their videos?

A Q W A R O Z Q E N V B
S (O) F D M I B V M N I X
K R D Q V A V L S (N) L Z
F E E D O Y X F N V L E
N R P I T S (E) D F T V E
N R Q S (W) P H R W K J F
H S (E) N G E O U J F E W
V N S (T) Q U N Z U X Y U
B Q N V S (U) D O B C F D
I G C Z E H Q E F E S B
E S (E) Q L J F A X B P Z
R G X Z M R U Y Q M V F

Write the circled letters here:

O N   E W E T U B E

Swim Team

Which one of these drawings is exactly the same as the ORIGINAL?
Look carefully and circle the one that is exactly the same.

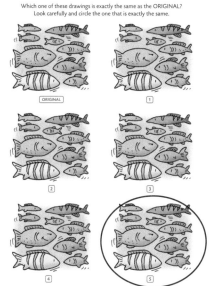

ORIGINAL   1
2   3
4   5

Teacher

What more noble job is there — spending day after day making
kids smarter and more interested in the world. Right?

Your job is to write down as many words as possible using just the letters in
TEACHER. No proper nouns and at least THREE letters long. OK, go!

HERE'S OUR LIST OF COMMON WORDS
If you think of others that are in the dictionary, count them!

ACE	TEA	HEAT	ERECT
ACT	TEE	HERE	HATER
ARC	THE	RACE	HEART
ARE	ACHE	RATE	REACH
ART	ACRE	TEAR	REACT
ATE	ARCH	THEE	TEACH
CAR	CARE	TREE	THERE
CAT	CART	CARET	THREE
EAR	CHAR	CATER	TRACE
EAT	CHAT	CHART	CREATE
ERA	EACH	CHEAT	HEATER
HAT	ETCH	CHEER	CHEATER
HER	HARE	CRATE	
RAT	HATE	EARTH	
TAR	HEAR	EATER	

U.S. States

Find and circle the 15 states
listed below. The hidden words can
read forward, backward, up, down,
and diagonally in all directions.

Salt Lake City   Augusta

K Y H A T U Y Y J M S R
Y E T D Y X N I T A O S
N N D I E P M V S C B Z
A E V R I L R N M N C V
G B K O E N A N D I W G
I R W L J K D W I F F O
H A Y F F U Y I A Z O J
C S O C C K I T A R A A
I K M O A D A V E N E O
M A I N E K Q G C X A Q
U H N N G E O R G I A Q
O J G S G N O P I E J S

IOWA	MAINE	NEVADA	GEORGIA	DELAWARE
OHIO	TEXAS	OREGON	INDIANA	MICHIGAN
UTAH	KANSAS	FLORIDA	WYOMING	NEBRASKA

138

Summer Fun

There are seven questions on the left, and seven joke answers on the right.
Match them up by writing the correct number in each space.

- Where do sharks go on vacation? **A. 4**
- Why don't mummies go on vacations? **B. 2**
- Why don't elephants buy suitcases for traveling? **C. 5**
- What does the Sun drink out of? **D. 7**
- What's the best day to get a sunburn at the beach? **E. 1**
- Where does a canoe go when it's not feeling well? **F. 3**
- Why did the miniature golfers bring extra socks? **G. 6**

1. Fry day.
2. They're afraid they'll relax and unwind.
3. To the dock.
4. Finland.
5. They already have trunks.
6. In case they get a hole in one.
7. Sun glasses.

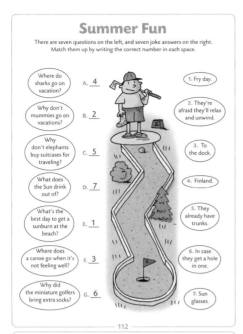

112

A Short Month

Put the 13 words into the grid in alphabetical order. We did the first one to get you started. Then write the highlighted letters from top to bottom in the spaces below to answer this joke:

Why did the guy get fired at the calendar factory?

FLOCK
BEGIN
ROBOT
WHIFF
DROVE
HIKED
CATER
JUDGE
PAYER
AHEAD
THEFT
IDEAL
MEALS

A	H	E	A	D
B	E	G	I	N
C	A	T	E	R
D	R	O	V	E
F	L	O	C	K
H	I	K	E	D
I	D	E	A	L
J	U	D	G	E
M	E	A	L	S
P	A	Y	E	R
R	O	B	O	T
T	H	E	F	T
W	H	I	F	F

Write the highlighted letters here:
H E   T O O K
A   D A Y   O F F

113

Tell a Phony

The answer to this joke is written using a simple code.

First, circle each letter that's immediately to the right of a P. We did the first one to get you started. Then write the circled letters (starting at the top and reading left to right) in the spaces below to answer this joke:

How do you figure out how old a smartphone is?

M F V R Q P (C) O R W K J
P (O) Z G V M O U J B F W
J Q N M T U P (U) V C E W
I G P (N) M H Q E S M E X
E M I Q L J U K P (T) Z A
B U X D O U M R K Q P (I)
Z Q P (T) B O L P (S) B M I
L S M N P (R) S R D Q R K
A P (I) S L Z M G E D O Y
X M E E Q E P (N) V I Z R
G X Z M R U Y Q M P (G) S
A M N P (S) U N Z U X Y U

Write the circled letters here:
C O U N T   I T S   R I N G S

114

Squirt Ahead

Find the one messy mustard path that runs from Start to End.
Go ahead. Show us you're a hot dog!

115

Various Vehicles

There are seven questions on the left, and seven joke answers on the right.
Match them up by writing the correct number in each space.

- Who DIDN'T invent the airplane? **A. 5**
- What did the tornado say to the car? **B. 1**
- What would you call a country where everyone drives red cars? **C. 7**
- What do you get if you group many houseboats together? **D. 2**
- What sound does a bulldozer make? **E. 6**
- How do trains hear each other? **F. 4**
- What has one horn and gives milk? **G. 3**

1. Want to go for a spin?
2. A township.
3. A milk truck.
4. With their engine-ears.
5. The wrong brothers.
6. The same as a cow that's dozing.
7. A red car-nation.

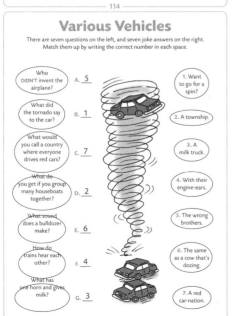

116

139

'Snow Joke

Put the 10 words into the grid in alphabetical order. We did the first one to get you started. Then write the highlighted letters from top to bottom in the spaces below to answer this joke:

What do you call a snowman in Florida?

KINGS
LAPEL
MOURN
FLUBS
BEACH
VALUE
YIELD
HABIT
PEDAL
RIDGE

B	E	A	C	H
F	L	U	B	S
H	A	B	I	T
K	I	N	G	S
L	A	P	E	L
M	O	U	R	N
P	E	D	A	L
R	I	D	G	E
V	A	L	U	E
Y	I	E	L	D

Write the highlighted letters here:
A   B I G
P U D D L E

117

Hammer Time

The answer to this joke is written using a simple code.

First, circle each letter that's immediately to the right of an H.
We did the first one to get you started. Then write the
circled letters (starting at the top and reading left to right)
in the spaces below to answer this joke:

What nail should you never hit with a hammer?

M F V R Q H Ⓨ O R W K J
H Ⓞ E N B O L P Z B M I
K Y Z G V M H Ⓤ J B F W
A H Ⓡ I H Ⓕ N Z U X Y U
B Q N M T U X H Ⓘ C E W
I G C H Ⓝ I Q E S M E X
E M I Q L H Ⓖ K X S Z A
A H Ⓔ S L Z M G E D O Y
X M E E Q E N R V H Ⓡ R
H Ⓝ Z M R U Y Q M S K S
C U H Ⓐ O U M R K Q O B
T S M H Ⓘ X S R D Q H Ⓛ

Write the circled letters here:

Y O U R   F I N G E R N A I L

118

Say Cheese!

Which one of these drawings is exactly the same as the ORIGINAL?
Look carefully and circle the one that is exactly the same.

119

140